▲

DOUGHNUTS AND DESTINY

Essays on the Psychology of Creativity

BRUCE HOLLY

▼

Copyright ©1995, Bruce Holly.

All rights reserved. No part of this book may be reproduced, stored in a retrieval or information system, or transmitted in any form or by any means, electronic, mechanical, photocopied, recorded, re-copied or re-typeset, or otherwise, without the written permission of the author, except in the case of brief excerpts in critical reviews and articles.

Published by Art Calendar Publishing, Inc.
P.O. Box 199
Upper Fairmount, MD 21867-0199
410-651-9150
Fax 410-651-5313

Printed in the United States of America

ISBN 0-945388-02-0

Library of Congress Catalog Card Number 95-075441

Cover Illustration:
River of Fortune, Photograph, 30"x24", ©1994, Michael Fatali, Page, Arizona.

*For Jane, Blaise, Lisa—
and my friends,
each of you.*

▲ Foreword

Usually when I read popular books on psychology I find myself mad as a wet cat, mired in "doing the work" the book is calling for, rehashing everything I've already forgiven everyone for, feeling sorry for the author, and wishing I'd been able to find a decent character-building novel instead.

Bruce's writing is different. We've had the privilege of publishing his column in our magazine every month since early 1990, and every time I finish typesetting one of his articles I breathe a thoughtful, satisfied "aaaah."

Don't get me wrong, I'm "doing the work" as I read Bruce's offerings too, but it *feels* different. Though I might shed tears while reading one of Bruce's pieces, what remains for me after reading his work is a sense of my spirit: dignity, clarity, and the inspiration and power to go create something.

When my husband-to-be introduced me to "Brucie" and his family in 1984, I was a professional pianist and a part-time emerging painter. After Drew and I married, sometimes when Bruce came to our house he would pull his abilities out of a secret pocket, like a precious gem. He would begin to muse over whatever painting I was working on at the time.

I was always impressed with his input. He gently gave me free family therapy through my painted portraits of my stepsons. He gave me sensitive critiques full of love and respect through my oils on panels. He offered the time line and the genogram tools, which are explained in this book better than I can summarize here.

Although Bruce offered his expertise freely, I valued it highly.

I started *Art Calendar*, "The Business Magazine for Visual Artists," in 1986. It was barely more than a newsletter when

Bruce M. Holly

it first came out—twenty pages of listings of professional opportunities for artists. But after a year or two of publishing *Art Calendar,* we started to add articles, and I asked Bruce to write a "Psychology of Creativity" column for us. I had a feeling he could write as well as he could critique in person. He said "Aw shucks," or something like that, but he came through with some of the most perfectly formed columns I have ever seen.

I hope you enjoy Bruce's observations as much as I have over the last several years. Bruce really is *good*, in person and on paper. Each essay in this book—a retrospective, if you will—is, in my estimation, a treasure. Allow yourself to hear Bruce, as you allow the sun to soak into your skin on those rare occasions when you let yourself sunbathe.

Carolyn Blakeslee Steis
Founding Editor
Art Calendar magazine

▲ Introduction

Several years ago, Bruce Holly began writing a monthly column for *Art Calendar* magazine. (Bruce, or perhaps his editor, identifies himself as a psychotherapist and artist, only not in that order.) His columns, which appear under the heading "The Psychology of Creativity," have been compiled in this book.

I am a psychiatrist, which explains how I know Bruce—we're colleagues. Also, I have picked up a paint brush from time to time. If Bruce weren't so tactful, he might describe my efforts as pretty little flowers. So the creative process, at least in terms of results, eludes me—but I can dream. And I am challenged by Bruce's writings on the subject.

Let me tell you something about the essays and a little more about the author.

Bruce Holly seems, at times, to be no ordinary mortal. He somehow has the ability to cram forty-eight hours into every twenty-four. He tells of sailing and motorcycling as if he has all the free time in the world. He paints, lectures, and writes. He treats patients. He's a capable, if reluctant, administrator. He shares anecdotes about his interactions with his son and daughter that reveal much about his role as father. And he reads—oh, how he reads. In these essays he quotes from such diverse sources as Kierkegaard, Piaget, Hawking, "Puff the Magic Dragon," and Jung, to whom he proffers folksy disagreement.

Most of Bruce's essays include ideas drawn from his training and experience as a psychotherapist. These are interwoven with parallels from the life of the artist. To do art, as he puts it, requires the courage to delve deeply into oneself, as does growth in psychotherapy. As only the truly mature and self-confident can do, Bruce—with self-deprecatory humor—shares with his readers his own fantasies, foibles, and failures.

He sometimes leads off with a personal story. He breaks his glasses miles from home; his boat capsizes in the middle of the Chesapeake Bay; he visits a gallery exhibition and relishes the food, drink, and friendship along with the art.

As with a good novel, one is immediately hooked into each essay. You may be struck by the imagery but not distracted from the good yarn. 'Long about the third paragraph, you might wonder, where on earth is he going with this? And what does it have to do with being creative?

It is a heretofore well-kept secret: sometimes Bruce didn't know the answers himself at that point in the writing.

But get there he does. Suddenly, you've been led into thoughtful, scholarly, and—yes—very serious stuff. Stuff like empathy, the meaning of meaning, the illusion of choice.

Bruce has a message, both for artists and for those of us who like to imagine that we are being creative once in a while. I think I heard the same message, a long time ago, from a Chinese analyst. Affecting broken English, he would gently say: "Insight fine—now what you goin' to do?"

Dorothy S. Dobbs, M.D.

God Goes Hunting, Acrylic on Canvas, 12"x8", ©1994, Bruce Holly

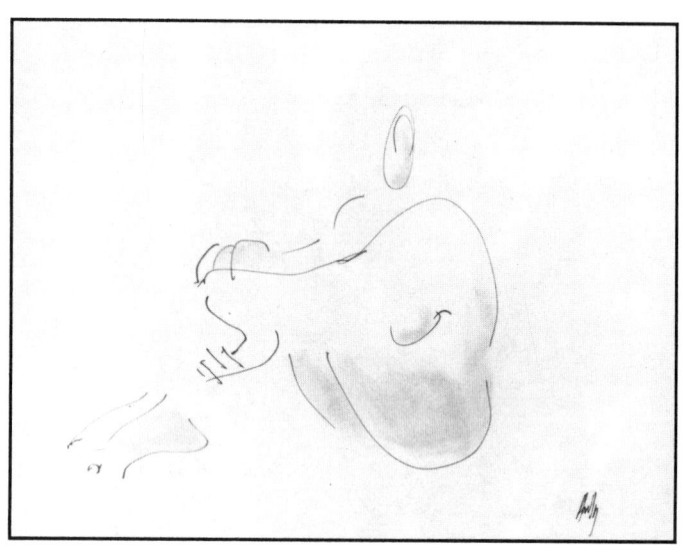

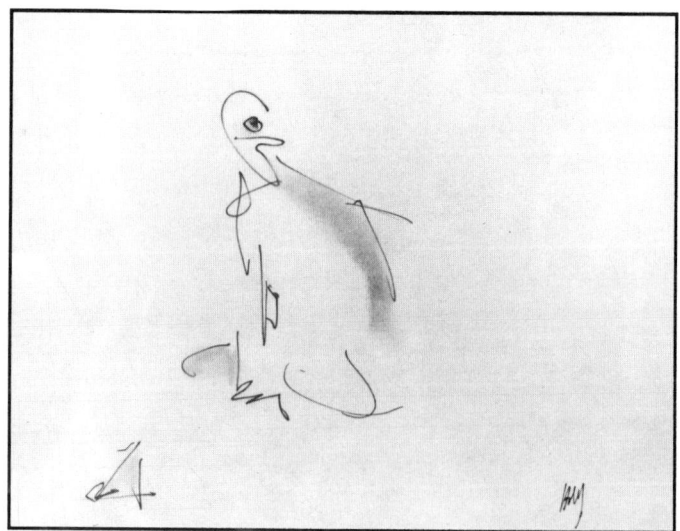

Gesture Drawings, Ink and Pastel on Paper,
18"x24", ©1978, Bruce Holly

▲ Experience

My son has taken to referring to me, lately, as "Old, slow, and gullible."

Heh, heh.

Not long ago, I mentioned to him, in the midst of one of our 1,500-miles-in-a-smelly-van-to-three-ski-areas-in-two-and-a-half-days spring ski marathon weekends, that when I was seventy I would get to ski for free.

"Neat," he said.

Then, I allowed, when I was seventy he would be forty, so he could do the driving.

That stopped him cold.

For the first time in his young life, it apparently sank in to him that I wasn't the only person in the crowd getting older. He looked at me with a stricken, my-world-has-just-changed-forever kind of expression. "I'll be *forty* when you're *seventy*? I don't *want* to be forty!"

Epiphany! Terror!

Recovery. With the eternal swiftness of youth, he shut the lid on the Pandora's box of reality he'd just peered into, and went on with his young, invincible, bulletproof, possibility-engorged life, oblivious to the slow, steady ticking beneath us all. And for the moment, so did I. Thank God.

As I write this, I'm thinking about friends and acquaintances for whom the box has been stuck in the full-open position for far too long, and for whom the ticking clock has become like a rushing thunder in their ears each moment of every day. For these folks, prayer takes the form of an ardent desire for their children, or themselves, to live long enough to have the privilege of becoming old, slow, and gullible.

Bruce M. Holly

Life is chancy, and it is itself a chance. As long as we keep on ticking, we have a chance to contribute new experience to each other. And our shared experience is, in the end, the precious ore we mine with our individual creativity. The artists among us are those who accept the task of describing complex convergences of experience in images that others can use to grow more aware of their own lives.

Art makes the intangible tangible; feeling becomes visible, thought becomes substance, and spirit is made concrete in a process of transubstantiation available to each of us in our own unique fashion. We can all become potential parents to a thousand creative births in ourselves and each other, every time we pick up a brush or chisel or etching tool.

As artists, we are forever standing in the midst of a roaring crossroads where past and future meet, and the known and unknown intersect. Sometimes we direct the traffic. Sometimes we simply witness the parade as it passes. And through our eyes, and ears, and hands, our fellows gain insight into what is going on.

However, like standing in a busy crossroads, artistic creativity is not without risk. Like a pedestrian at rush hour, an artist needs freedom of movement, courage, and self-awareness to survive; while artists serve as conduits for the complex truth of every instant to emerge into the light of common knowledge, we sometimes also serve as lightning rods for the furious energy of a universe still awkwardly unfolding.

Additionally, art is full of rules to be obeyed or broken in the service of our efforts to transcend the bonds of time, space, and social convention that otherwise bind our every minute. Thus, we often stand out for our willingness to deviate from the norm as much as for our visions of the new. And in the heavy traffic of life, deviance is dangerous. In the end, few activities are as valuable as art in the ongoing history of mankind, or as demanding.

What wonders my son and daughter stand to learn with a little age on them. Their aches and pains and bumps and scars will serve as their admission tickets to the richest source of wisdom and meaning that I know of: experience. As they grow, they will have to decide, as we all do, a thousand times a day, whether or not they will try something new, or explore a different path, or push themselves further along a hard way. More and more, they will have to rely on their own judgment about which choices they make in each instance. And with each moment they will reap both the consequences and the learning contained in each decision. I hope they will also choose to share what happens in their own creative work.

I wish them well, and I'm doing everything I know of to prepare them as well as I can, and so is their mother. Up until now, while we've made most of the choices for them, we've tried to teach them how to make choices by letting them in on our thinking. We've tried to model how to take risks, and tough as it is, we've tried to let them know what happens when things haven't gone our way in some of those decisions. And now, as they are getting older, we're struggling with the hardest job I have yet run into as a parent: letting them fly on their own.

Initially, their awkward flapping might be ineffectual, yet were they only to glide they would surely lose height. I hope they learn to flap hard when they have to, so they can soar as high or glide as much as they might wish. In the end, though, the course of their flight is up to them—and the wind.

Old, slow, and gullible. That phrase is beginning to define my goal in life, and my wish for my children. I want to be ancient, to have seen it all. I want to be slow, because rushing speed must take its own toll, and youth is when I was better prepared to pay it—so that now, with experience, I can see how much time there really is between each moment that seemed so fleeting before.

And gullible—I want to be able to believe more often than not in my brothers and sisters, and in God, and in tomorrow. So far, good.

Enjoy, kids.

▲ THRESHOLDS

Each of us has our own secret ceremonies for standing on the threshold of change. Some of us stand naked in the dawn, as lonely as we can ever be, waiting for the moment when we move into our future, the moment that puts us "on the road." Others of us gather a crowd to attend our rituals of beginning. We want to share the tension out, feeding on the courage of the group to get ourselves over our personal thresholds and into unexplored territory.

Thresholds abound around us. The present forms a boundary beyond which all time waits in a future with limits we do not comprehend. Our every movement crosses a threshold which changes our point of view in a universe where everything around us is inexorably moving in its own right. And then, there is the threshold of our own fear of the unknown, the new, the emotional land beyond our familiar limits.

The word "threshold" in its archaic origins probably described a sill fashioned at the edge of an area where kernels of edible grains, such as wheat, were knocked loose, or threshed, apart from the inedible parts of the plant. These sills served to keep the grain within the confines of the threshing floor so it could be gathered together more easily.

Thus, thresholds existed initially to contain. And so they do today, in a broader sense. People speak of thresholds of pain, of endurance, of patience—within these kinds of thresholds, most of us present similar images to ourselves and each other, our behavior generally rational, conforming to societal norms, predictable, and generally unremarkable.

In its more modern usage, the word "threshold" indicates a boundary which, when crossed, marks a substantial change in condition. On one side of such a boundary, one is usually safe, comfortable, within specifications, acceptable, and so on. On the other side of such a boundary, one is beyond the pale, in the "red zone," at risk—beyond the edge, so to speak.

Most of us learn what our approximate thresholds of emotional and physical ability and comfort are, and tend to go through life playing it safe, keeping well within these boundaries on a normal day-to-day basis. In fact, after a while many of us treat these thresholds as rigid limits, boundary lines to be avoided for the most part and kept at a respectful distance, much like electric fencing. We tend to forget that in themselves, our thresholds are simply demarcation lines in our experience which signal us that beyond them lie parts less familiar, less comfortable at times, often deeper in emotional intensity, and less consciously in control than we are used to dealing with in ourselves.

Some of us are especially cautious, and spend most of our lives in the middle of our personal threshing floors, beating the fruit of our lives that is within easy, safe reach carefully into neat, small piles, well inside the limits of our known selves.

Others of us, some of the most troubled of us, compulsively travel only the outer rim of our safety zones at the edges and beyond of our personalities and personal control, beating ourselves as if driven by demons to do so, strewing whatever learning, whatever meaning, whatever sanity we might otherwise have into the darkness beyond recovery, lost to ourselves and our fellow men. The novel, the unique, the intense in our experiences is scattered like errant radiation rather than formed creatively into communication which adds to our lives and the life of the world.

And, there are some of us who can cover the whole floor, as it were. We can move creatively well within our personal limits, and we can move out, gathering what is to be gained at the edges of our comfort, shaking as much truth out of our outlying experience as we can, even at risk of needing on occasion to step out beyond the boundaries of our pain or fear or doubt to collect it once it is shaken loose.

What is beyond those boundaries, those personal thresholds we often fear so much? What is so powerful about the unknown that contemplating it can sometimes throw us into panic, the disorganization of our wits that renders us so helpless to help ourselves at least for the moment?

Really. Ask *yourself* this question: "What *is* to fear?"

In asking yourself what is to fear, you take the very first, so very necessary, step in making it unlikely that what you now fear will ever again terrify you into helplessness.

What is so frightening about the unknown? You want a powerful mantra, words to guide you through life? Here it is: "What, *exactly*, am I afraid of here?"

Ask this question at every possible turn, and you will find yourself moving boundaries that today seem like impenetrable walls, into parts of your experience that at this moment are far beyond your awareness. For most of us, in many situations, the rational, truthful answer is: "I don't know what I'm afraid of." And pushing further, the "I don't know" becomes "I'm afraid of *what* I don't know."

Guess what? We don't know *most* things.

Guess what, again. Most things, when you actually encounter them—are benign.

Life tends *not* to be filled with sharp points and rough edges, for most of us, even though it often feels that way for a lot of us.

I believe life has a few really smooth, warm, comfortable passages, a lot of generally neutral ground, and a bit of really rough terrain, myself.

If you are a betting person (and any sentient being is), betting at least part of the rent on the next few minutes of your life being at least a bit pleasant is usually a fairly safe wager. Even in the hard stretches.

In my line of work, I find myself often engaged in helping people weather the hard parts of their lives by appreciating, at the very least, the beauty and power of the tools they have to cope with difficulty. It seems *recognizing* one's strength is a *source* of strength for a lot of people.

So too in one's creative life. Every canvas, every block of stone or wood, every blank page or videotape, every lump of clay—all are thresholds. That we even stand at the edge of such creative boundaries is a measure of our creative courage. That we *move* to enter into the unknown images contained within these waiting spaces and volumes, and with our creative tools allow these images a life of their own—that is the measure of us as artists. We not only stand at the threshold of creativity, we risk crossing it.

▲ On Creative Block

Recently, I received something very precious—useful criticism. A few weeks after I'd spoken to a local art association, I called the woman who had organized things and asked for her comments. I heard two observations: I hadn't talked loudly enough for everyone to hear, and I hadn't answered the practical questions many people had come to hear me address—mostly about working through or around creative blocks.

These days, talking to groups has become a clear gamble, for me and for the group that asks me to speak. I used to think I could speak well, with wit, animation, and some sense that I knew what I was talking about. Nowadays, things still go well sometimes—I say things that meet what the audience needs, and they and I enjoy the experience. Things "click." On other occasions, things go "clunk," and both I and my audience find ourselves disappointed. Sometimes I'm off because I'm nervous, uptight, confronting my own demons of fear and foolishness. But sometimes, I think it's because I make some assumptions that turn out to be incorrect. For example, I will assume that what I have to say about being productive is already common knowledge amongst artists, or so simple as to be simplistic. Or that because it has been said or written about before, it doesn't need saying again.

I wonder where I got such strange ideas, as I write them now. I know enough about how humans learn and work to realize that while these assumptions are all true—that we as artists do "know" what we have to do to produce work, that the basic principles that lead to creativity are "simple," and that most of us have heard the ideas expressed before—the ideas are worth hearing again and again.

Bruce M. Holly

All good speakers and teachers know these things. What makes some speakers stand out, however, is that they convey these ideas with a personal conviction and clarity that allows their audience to respond with their own creative action. And the key word here is and always has been: "action."

It is possible to frame the notion of a creative block as a creative choice to make a personal statement by avoiding action. (But one must realize: it's been done before, and isn't very creatively unique.) As much as it feels like an inability, it is a choice.

There. We have confronted the hardest part of the truth about blocks. We consciously or unconsciously *choose* to be unproductive. Believe that, and if you are struggling with a creative block, you are at the crux of your problem, and ready to deal with and resolve the reasons why.

And dealing with the causes is another choice. Another truth: each action leads to *another* choice, "Do I *keep* acting?"

The blocks most of us stumble against in art are made from the clay of our own experience. We may butt up against walls which separate us from our desire to create and swear by all that is holy that we are mystified by why they are there. But they are there for reasons, and they have to do with our needs, our ways of defending ourselves, and the unconscious influences that shape each of our lives in powerful ways.

There are several possibilities for removing these blocks. The most obvious—we can wait them out, or grind through them. Most of us slow down or slide to a temporary halt on occasion, often when we are fatigued or distracted by events of everyday life—births, deaths, anniversaries, disappointments, love affairs, and the like. When circumstances change, or we get enough rest, we get back to work fairly easily. Or if we've been grinding along, the work becomes easier.

We can use our own resources—introspection, constructive criticism, brainstorming with friends—to search out the reasons for blockage. The reasons might not be

Essays on The Psychology of Creativity

obvious, but are waiting to be noticed, to dawn on us if we let them—boredom, insecurity, anger at ourselves or others, disappointment with our creative direction, and so on. In these cases, the resolution of the block comes from putting our finger on the source of creative discomfort, and addressing it through consciously changing direction, resolving a specific conflict, or developing needed skills.

Or we can suspect that in some cases, the very mystery and strength of the blocks suggest that they are serving a defensive purpose, buffering us from awareness of aspects of our lives that would feel overwhelming to us if they were to be expressed. In these cases, the usefulness of a personal psychotherapy is not to be underestimated. The forces which are acting to thwart creativity may feel overwhelming but once brought to light and explored in a supportive relationship with a sensitive therapist, they can become a vast source of new creative energy.

How do you tell what you need to do? By using a simple yardstick. If you can act creatively at all, you are not blocked. But more relevantly, if your work takes an inordinate amount of will and energy to do, and does not respond to your efforts to wait the difficulty out or work it through on your own, and if you are truly blocked rather than simply uncommitted to doing art, therapy is the way to go.

This particular essay comes with a guarantee. If you do the following things, you will become a producing artist. Your art may be different, at least for a while, than what you want it to be, or it may be unpleasing to you, or unpredictable ... but, you *will* be productive.

1. Get started. Do something, anything. Right now. If you are a painter, drop this book, get your paints and make a mark on whatever you use, paper, canvas, whatever. If you are a sculptor, go find a chunk of something and give it a judicious whack. If you are a choreographer, get up and move. Just do it.

2. Once you've started, keep something going, all the time. Get in the habit of starting something new while you're still working on something else. I've taken up using my leftover paint mixings for one piece to start another canvas, kind of like sourdough starter.

3. Promise yourself you'll take a risk each time you work on a piece. Deliberately cause yourself some trouble on at least one piece each time you work. Then work it out. You can always throw it out. But don't.

4. Cezanne took the attitude that each painting was "research." Take the same attitude. Learn something new. It's there. Honest. In each piece. Look for it.

5. Never "finish" a piece. Just allow yourself to stop somewhere. Picasso knew this, now you do.

6. Look. Study. Think. Always, always keep a pencil and paper with you. Use them a lot. Record thoughts, images, details—for no specific reason. Write legibly.

7. Pay attention to the little thoughts, the subtle "self-talk" you're doing in the back of your mind about what you shouldn't or can't do. Write these thoughts down as you become aware of them, and examine each, mechanically asking yourself the question "What if the opposite is true?" Then, try doing the opposite, and pay attention to what happens inside you and in the art you produce.

8. Realize that each piece says something to someone. Never underestimate this. No message is unworthy of respect for this reason.

9. Find people who appreciate what you are doing in your art. Show them your work, and use what they say—not as gospel, but as energy.

10. Think of your life as a work of art, the result of a series of choices leading to action. Document it as much as you can.

▲ Subtle Perspectives

I have two recurring fantasies. The first is that God has a sense of humor—at times unfathomable to us, at times apparently cruel beyond words—and at other times, so rich and subtle, so elegant, so kind and self-effacing that the only possible response for us is to cry with delight. A God in love with irony. A God who occasionally lets us in on the joke. A God whose chuckles, chortles, and howls are almost audible in just about everything we do.

I thought about this fantasy today. It was a warm, moody gray day in Washington, and I was wrapped up tighter than usual, feeling put-upon and sorry for myself, barking at my children, yapping at my wife—so I went sailing. It was a gorgeous day for it, given that it was early March. It was so pleasant, in fact, that almost immediately after launching my boat and sailing into the Potomac, I felt guilty for having left my family behind, instead of righteously selfish, as I'd hoped to feel. I sailed on, grumbling to myself and realizing that my escape was becoming a penance.

Just as I arrived at the cove where I was intending to moor for a while and sulk, weather appropriate to my feelings came my way. I changed plans, dropped sail, and motored back upriver in a veritable vale of tears, a steady succession of gusty squalls and drizzle that cooled both my ardor for sailing in March and my anger.

Finally, back at the launching ramp as I disappointedly splashed around between attacks of shivering to get the boat back on the trailer, I glanced down to find a quarter in the water. I scooped it up with eager, albeit damp, glee.

At that point, the day seemed scripted like a morality tale written by a little kid, and it occurred to me that God probably giggles like a five-year-old when He creates such scenes. In any case, I drove home a bit less grouchy, and a bit wiser. And a little bit richer too.

My other fantasy is that my own personal reason for being alive is so subtle that neither I nor anyone else will ever know it—that, for instance, one afternoon, as I'm taking a walk after a rain shower, my shadow will glide over a puddle, blocking out the reflected glare of an emerging sun a split second before it would have blinded a passing truck driver, rendering him unable to see a woman wheeling a baby carriage into his path; the woman and child will survive as a result, and the child will grow up to be the great-great grandmother of the architect of final, just, and lasting world peace. I will have existed in order to cast one shadow at the right time. As fantasies go, this is only just mildly megalomaniac, by the way.

In times of trouble, these fantasies comfort me. They somehow reassure me of things I do not know, but believe exist—the meaning of all life, the inherent orderliness of chaos, the truth in the wind. I replay them in my mind at odd moments, and like soft music, or snippets of comforting early memories, my feelings and perspective on the immediate present are affected, at least a little. And that little bit is what it takes to keep on.

There is a technique used in hypnosis called reframing. Basically what you do is invite someone to see, or hear, or feel, or understand something from a perspective different than the one he or she has been using. For instance, instead of understanding one's fear as an impediment to change, one can see it as a useful ally in moving carefully; anger can often be recast as forceful caring; pain can be experienced as reassurance that you are still alive, and so on—the once half empty cup becomes seen as almost full. Some might call this self-delusion; others might call it positive thinking. The point that seems useful is that many if not most experiences can have more than one meaning, depending on one's attitude toward them.

Henry Moore wrote in *Notes on Sculpture* that "It is a mistake for a sculptor or a painter to speak or write very often about his job. It releases tension needed for his work." I'll risk it now, though.

I have two small paintings going on. One is of an image that emerged while I was doodling, pushing pigment around on a canvas. The other is an image I've had in mind for some time now, and drew out on the canvas a couple of years ago.

I can easily understand where the emergent image came from. It is of a man lying against a tree by a brook amidst flowers and grass.

I used to paint large, violent canvases. At the time I was young and felt violently. Because, in part, I wanted to paint "pretty," I quit painting for a long time. This is the first painting I've started in quite a while. It is not a pretty picture. So it goes. There's a part of me that's not done being young and violent and uncomfortable.

The man is intended to be self-content, comfortable in his solitude, and relaxed. But the colors and the brushwork are tense and strong and thick and tumultuous. The trees are barren, twisted olive trunks reaching skyward. The figure is layered with colors, and the effect, incomplete as the picture is, is discomfiting, a vision of unresolved strata not quite hidden from view.

I could be disappointed in it. It's not the picture I'd hoped to paint. It comforts me though, to look at it as an image of myself as a work in progress, still incomplete, and in transition. It, and I, can change, and will change. That's nice for a forty-one-year-old to keep in mind at times.

The other picture, the one that began with a pencil sketch, is equally unfinished, and in some ways less defined than the picture of the man. However, it seems to me equally powerful and personally evocative. I notice a certain objective distance in how I'm working on it—a kind of professional reserve, you might say. The image is of an old woman, seated by a high stone wall, beneath an encroaching, heavily-leaved tree. In the figure of the woman, as of now the least-defined portion of the painting, I see warmth and resignation; the wall behind her seems to me less a barrier or obstacle than a last boundary between her and the infinity of the sky.

It is, as I see it, a picture of life and the end of life, and resonates with a part of me that begins, as I get older, to be less afraid of death—particularly that of my parents, and also, my own. This picture too will change before it is finished. In a way, this one is a "pretty" picture in the making.

On both pictures, things are going slowly. I'm battling with a fear familiar to many of us, it turns out—I don't want to screw up the parts of the picture that please me during various stages of its evolution.

I'm struck with how many artists specifically talk about needing to destroy even the good on the way to a work's final evolution. In a conversation in 1934 with Christian Zervos, Picasso observed, "When one begins a picture one often discovers fine things. One ought to beware of these, destroy one's picture, recreate it many times. On each destruction of a beautiful find, the artist ... transforms it, condenses it, makes it more substantial." Moreover, according to Picasso, "The nail is the undoer of painting .... The day it is bought and hung on the wall ... the painting is done for."

I had a studio partner and friend, Ulysses Marshall, who often used his old canvases over and over, with underlying images becoming part of the immediate moment's work. Each painting had its own internal history, some of which was visible at any given moment. I recently heard of a sculptor who occasionally does house calls on pieces he's sold, to "update" them.

For creative people, the ability to finish a work of art is often more like recognizing a good stopping point on a hike filled with good stopping points, than it is like reaching the end of the trail. And the difference between a stopping point and a sticking point in art is often simply a subtle variation in perspective, that allows you to see that the trail could continue if you wanted to follow it further.

▲ The Heart of It

At first, I didn't worry too much about what was in the offing. My daughter's school was sponsoring an art auction by a large commercial dealer as a fund-raiser. I was one of the volunteer laborers who turned out early one Saturday morning to help set the thing up. I figured it would at the very least be an interesting day, an opportunity to see a little art, watch people throw a few bucks at some offset prints, have a few drinks, and eat like a horse. I didn't figure on going through a major existential crisis, a trauma of the soul, which, by the end of the evening, is what I later figured out had happened to me.

Oh, my dear Lord. What happened was astounding.

A van rolled up, filled with framed pieces, fresh from what I now imagine is a vast warehouse somewhere in the heart of darkness in UPS Zone Two. A young man began handing us pictures off the back and we humped them into a large hall filled with tables against the wall. As we carried the stuff in and leaned it on the tables, it became apparent to me that the pictures were not my cup of tea. Most were prints, parts of huge editions, some signed. Some of the pictures were originals, the kind of art you might see on a movie set replicating the interior of a stereotypical Middle-American white-bread home. Stylized Caucasian-looking women in kimonos with their bare backs "S"-curving through the center of the pictures, a series of brightly-colored neo-primitive American town scenes, the odd smattering of Norman Rockwell offset prints of Tom Sawyer *et al*. That kind of thing.

I figured I would at least eat well during the evening. I knew then I wouldn't be spending much on art that night, and I figured that anyone dropping more than thirty or forty dollars on any of the pieces would be doing so out of a charitable heart, and would be likely to be a little morose as well as hung over the next morning. They'd at least get a fairly decent frame out of the deal.

Oh, my dear Lord. How out of touch could I be?

That evening, my wife, a couple of friends and I showed up. So had several hundred other folks. I grabbed a beer and a handful of cheese and bread, and looked around again. I was mildly surprised at the apparent level of interest many of the people were showing in the art. Egocentric as I am, it's always at least a mild surprise when it dawns on me that my likes and dislikes aren't necessarily shared by every other member of the human race.

Soon, an auctioneer appeared up on the stage at the front of the room—a handsome dark-haired devil (Mephisto?!)—resplendent in a shiny black tux and a lapel brooch, for heaven's sake. He began by explaining the drill for the evening and making a bit of light banter. By this time, I was getting a bit stupefied on beer and cheese and the general scene, and both awed and appalled at the notion that apparently there were people who *liked* some of the pieces on display.

(Technique Number One: Give 'em time to have a couple of drinks before starting—it loosens things up.)

Mr. Mephisto soon proved himself a consummate master of orchestration, timing, and psychology—a Master Salesman! I became fascinated, repulsed, awed, overwhelmed. He started off with a few small prints of Norman Rockwell illustrations.

(Technique Number Two: Nothing too hard at first— make it easy to get the first bid.)

Somebody started bidding as if by reflex, and someone else jumped in, and we were off for the evening, it looked like. No real surprises yet. A comfortable, cheery evening, watching a master at work, and nice people being a little bit generous so the school would be able to roll in a little dough.

Then things began to get really weird, really fast, at least for me.

After a couple of small sales, Mephisto signalled to his cronies to set up one of the larger Kimono Lady paintings on the auction block. Then—and this sends chills down my spine—he ... began ... to explain why this picture was ... IMPORTANT!

Oh, my dear, dear Lord.

(Technique Number Three: Tell 'em why they should BUY THIS PICTURE!)

He said things that had to do with "... Number One painter of this genre at the moment ... Note the poodle in the corner—the most valuable and collectible images he's painted all have poodles in them ... He's our most popular artist this year ... and, we have a buy-back policy!"

I was in a swoon.

Then the world got even more intensely strange—he announced the minimum opening bid—$9,200!

I felt disembodied, like I was floating around observing myself in a scene from the depths of a schizophrenic seizure—what the hell was going on? Where is the meaning here? Am I nuts, or what? The piece was something I would not be able to tolerate in my house for ten minutes. It was, in my view, likely the ten-thousandth in a series of repetitive, bland, clichéd, trivial, no-account chicken-art simulations that are to art as a two-minute five-dollar quickie in a doorway is to making love.

And then, the numbing, predictable, banal, inevitable next event: people actually bid on the thing, and someone—a merciful God will keep his awesome idiocy intact—actually bought the thing for several hundred dollars more than the initial bid.

(Technique Number Four: Land a big one early enough to influence the rest of the fish to bite big.)

The rest of the evening was anticlimactic. I don't remember much else, except for the occasional phrase from Mephisto as he described the "worth" of subsequent pieces: "... This one has a lot of green in it. It would go well in a green room ... A charming piece. Paintings this size usually sell for $400 ..."

I left feeling like I had been at a slave auction. What should have been an evening filled with soul and heart and magic was more like watching wretched, painted waifs being peddled like so much dried meat. I could not believe my response, given that in my line of work I tend to see some massively strange and crazy situations as a matter of daily routine. Until this particular evening, I had a sense that I understood what "beyond belief" meant. I now have a new understanding.

Creative art, in my mind, is anything done by a human being that goes one stroke beyond the functional. But understand the word "functional" in this context: phony, crass, and dastardly functional pseudo-art abounds, ranging from the black-velvet metallic paint Big-Eyed Elvis paintings that some poor *campesino* in Juarez knocks out for a few cents for someone to sell at your local gas station to the slickest of gallery-packaged well-framed torn-paper abstracts that sell big-time uptown. The function these serve is to be "valuable," their meaning convertible into some form of exchange—money, prestige, power—for someone, be it the maker, the seller, or the buyer. Their intrinsic value as living expressions of a human heart or psyche is, and always has been from their conception, *secondary* to being "valuable."

Friends, never ever underestimate the art market. In fact, I would at this point say it is impossible to underestimate what can be sold. But never, ever confuse success in the market with a means for measuring creative worth.

As for me, I've decided I clearly can't handle warehouse-packaged fund-raising art auctions. The experience is much too intense for me.

But—wait! Of course! The power of it all! It's taken me until this very moment to realize ... this is the only way I can make sense of it ... the whole auction was a powerful piece of *performance* art. It had to be. It just had to be. It *must* have been somebody's genius statement about the valuation of art, about the perception of "art," about the monstrous capacity of well-intentioned people to tear the living soul out of even the holiest endeavors.

Now I feel better.

Next time, though, I'll volunteer to set up a Tupperware party instead.

▲ Inner Voices

At times, I am clinically "social phobic." That is, I suffer from an exaggerated fear of being evaluated or judged by others, and an intense desire to avoid scrutiny. So why do I write and paint and lecture? All of these activities are at best challenging, and at worst, excruciating for me.

The obvious answer is the right one, for me: I want the rewards these activities bring me, and I'm willing to pay the price for them. But why is the price so high?

Most people tighten up a bit when they face situations where they expect others to evaluate their performance, even when there is no question that they are talented and competent. Most are able to tolerate the discomfort and perform in spite of it, and with time and experience the feeling diminishes. What allows this to happen?

Artists, probably more than most people, face the fear of being scrutinized and found wanting. We face it in many contexts: in our definitions of ourselves as artists; in what we show of ourselves and our creative and technical competence in each work we turn out; in our efforts to have our work seen and understood; and our efforts to learn and expand our work. We draw, paint, write, dance, play music. We subject our work to the criticism of peers and critics. We mail off slides and carry portfolios around to galleries in hopes of acceptance. We give talks about our art. Some of us enjoy the interchange, and learn from it. Others of us cannot hear much of it: for some, praise falls on deaf ears, and for others criticism is ignored as irrelevant, even when it is warranted and could be useful. Many of us so fear the risks involved that we avoid these situations completely, hoping all the while for someone like an agent or benefactor who will see our talent and protect us from all the pain involved in looking for an appreciative audience.

Our images of ourselves develop over time, beginning early in our lives. At first, we are helpless and almost totally dependent on our mothers and fathers, or their stand-ins. If during this period we are fed with attention and care when we are hungry, we begin to learn that we can expect attention and care as a given. If we are comforted when we are frightened, we learn that even fear can be dealt with. If we are encouraged and praised when we take our first steps in the world, we keep on walking, despite stumbles and bumps.

On the other hand, to the extent that no mother or father is perfect, we also learn that sometimes life is unpredictable, unfair, painful, and scary, and we won't always be rescued or even supported in our struggles. Sometimes we will even be blamed or criticized for having been inadequate or foolish. Sometimes we will be left to learn alone from our experience. And sadly, sometimes, some of us are abandoned at an early age to fend for ourselves emotionally, or even targeted as the cause of our parents' problems. Overwhelming guilt is a painful but common legacy in many families.

As we grow, many people enter our lives in the posture of parents: teachers, friends, lovers, critics, bosses. We tend to try to make life understandable by making it familiar, so we tend to expect these folks to act like the parents of our early experience, or we wishfully expect them to fill every deficiency and void in that experience. In either case, the present becomes shaped by the past. Sometimes, our wishes come true to some extent: our accumulated experience with people who accept and respond helpfully to us allows us to see ourselves as capable, lovable, and potent human beings, and we begin to act that way. Often, however, we are so attuned to what we have learned to expect, and so anxious or resigned to it, that our perceptions are distorted. Instead of having new experiences, we have old experiences repeated over and over with different players.

Margot Adler, a reporter with National Public Radio, recently said of a man she interviewed, "Like a survivor of an earthquake, he has learned to walk while trembling." Humans are resilient beings, from infancy. We can survive a lot. We require only adequate, not perfect, parenting in order to make our way in the world. We are all born innocent and lovable, and creatively potent. How much of that innocence, love, and potency survives into our adult lives is a function not only of the adequacy of our early experience, but of our own ability to understand that experience and modify its impact on ourselves.

An artist friend of mine refers to having "critical parents" inside her as she works or writes or speaks; they influence how she feels about herself, and at times seem to almost kill the joy she feels in being a creative person. Psychoanalysts have long described how we seem to internalize our parents' images and directives at an early age, and how these internalized perceptions continue to guide and influence our thoughts and feelings throughout later life. More recently, persons recovering from alcohol and other substance abuse have often used a related metaphor of the "inner child" in each of us who continues to need and seek nurturing and attention in our adult lives as a result of our childhood experiences.

It is as if we unconsciously retain our perspectives as small children in our adult lives. We respond to internal voices which make us feel good or bad, secure or shameful, competent or inept. The voices we "hear" can be helpful and energizing, or they can be resolutely critical, abusive, or fearful, chanting: "You can't, you shouldn't, you'll fail" at every opportunity. They can be conditional: "If you don't do things my way, whatever you do is bad." They can be pervasive: "You've always been clumsy in everything you do, and you'll always be that way."

Cognitive therapists such as Aaron Beck postulate that thoughts like these flash across our minds as we prepare to take action, and give rise to anxiety and irrational fear. As a result, we struggle harder than necessary, or we misread the reality around us, resulting in over- or under-reaction to it. Once we become aware of these distortions and misperceptions, however, we can correct them. In effect, we can change the "tapes" we listen to about ourselves, and free ourselves for new behavior.

How can you begin to help yourself? First of all, take inventory of the beliefs you have about yourself. For instance, you can do this by tuning in to the thoughts you have just before trying something new. Listen to whether you start off sentences about yourself with "I can't ..., I shouldn't ..., I don't ...".

Next, question each and every one of these beliefs as you become aware of them. Ask yourself: "What if I said the opposite about myself?" Then do so, and see what happens.

Finally, be very curious about where these beliefs and attitudes have come from. Trace them back to where, when, and from whom you first learned them. And when you have done so, realize that if an attitude or feeling you are studying diminishes you in any way, this in itself is a signal that it arose out of a mistake someone made rather than a useful observation, and you now can correct that mistake for yourself. It does not matter that you have lived with it for a long time because your mother or father made it when you were a child, or an inept teacher did it in junior high school, or your friend did it yesterday. What matters is that you recognize it as a distorting, limiting factor in your life today. Now you have an opportunity to choose new perspectives to live by—a chance to be your own "nurturing parent."

▲ In the Background, Constantly

If I could have a background soundtrack for the day-to-day happenings of my life—like the music in a movie that serves as accompaniment for the action—I'd really be in high cotton. Life could be so much richer if we all had such soundtracks that matched our feelings, or the tension of the situations we were in, or the mood of the hour—music that we could turn up or down depending on how aware of it we wanted to be, or how much we wanted it to tip off others to what we were feeling at the moment. Imagine! Beethoven at the beach! Brahms at breakfast! Blondie in bed! Grateful Dead in bed! The New York Philharmonic in bed!

Picture this: you walk into a party. The William Tell Overture is playing softly around you. You look around in mild anticipation—something good may happen here tonight. A small clot of young men are in animated conversation on the deck, and the brassy sophistication of melodies in the air suggests money games—they are stockbrokers. By the bar, a boozy but boring clarinet riff warns you that your next-door neighbor has had a bit too much and has launched into a far-too-familiar story about his last vacation. In a far corner, a couple is talking animatedly—and the barely audible strains of the banjo duel from "Deliverance" keep most people a safe distance away from them.

And then—there, in the open doorway of the kitchen! How long has it been? She looks around. She looks at you! She tilts her head ever so slightly and recognition washes across her eyes like a tide—the years fall away, and you float toward each other, the roaring crescendo of "The Hallelujah

Chorus" around you both, rising to drown the rest of the world out. All in the party turn to the sound, to witness the moment. Life is good! ALLELUIA! ALLELUIA! AL-LE-LU-IAHHHH!

And then, the moment passes. The banjo begins to play again, over in the darkness. An animated babble of jazz, soft rock, and elevator music picks back up. You reach for a canape. You hear the soft sounds of "My Boyfriend's Back" next to you ... Yes! It *is* going to be quite a party!

Now I'm enough a part of the twentieth century to know that many of us supply such backgrounds for ourselves using boom boxes or bass blasters. But I'm talking about *everybody, all the time, everywhere*. There would be a constant murmur of music throughout the world, like the sound of millions of radios tuned to different stations and turned on low, with occasional eccentrics turned loud enough to stand out a bit on the odd beats. On rare occasions, the sound would mesh, and on rarer occasions still, the sounds would largely match-- say, at the news of the death of Mother Teresa, or on a smaller scale, at the moment of simultaneous orgasm.

Such a phenomenon would certainly help us deal with the risky bits of life, at least some of the time. When I was a kid at a horror movie, I'd listen for the ominous measures that let me know something was coming, something horrible, something that was ... almost ... HERE! Aaughh! But by the time it appeared onscreen, I'd be safe under my jacket, watching through the sleeve. That's the kind of warning I want in life, darn it.

And think how we could more closely and accurately gauge our impact upon each other. This would be no small plus for speakers, teachers, salesmen, lovers, or artists of any stripe.

Here's the punchline of all this. We *do* have these "soundtracks" going, constantly. Stop for a moment, and you will become aware of yours. It might not be music, though.

What defines our present experiences and interprets them, provides us with early warnings of things to come or things already afoot around us, and serves to clue others in to our moods, frames of mind, or attitudes—and does this constantly, twenty-four hours a day—is our shared unconscious life, an amalgam of perceptions, thoughts, feelings, and behaviors far more complicated than music alone.

Synesthesia is a process most of us experience only occasionally on a conscious level. In essence, the boundaries between our senses disappear and we "see" sounds, or "hear" colors, or "feel" tastes, for example. On the other hand, synesthesia abounds in our unconscious lives—which is to say, it abounds in the greater part of our living experience. This is demonstrated in the common languages of emotion that inform all our arts, and it is this synesthetic process which allows us to share these languages between us. Thus, dance can serve as an intelligible expression of feeling in movement; visual art can communicate meaning in color and line; and music and poetry can result from emotions perceived as sound and rhythm. Moreover, it is largely through this unconsciously occurring dissolution of the boundaries between our physical senses that we gain intuition, the ability to perceive and often accurately interpret the meanings in relationships and events that occur beneath the spoken words or visible events.

So, then, our personal soundtracks are more accurately described as Sensurround experiences, with every nerve ending we own constantly responding to our lives in an interpretive manner, both internally and externally. To the extent that we can pay conscious attention to this aspect of our experience, and perceive it occurring in our brothers and sisters, we have the same sort of accompaniment, early warning, and release that any soundtrack ever provided for a movie.

Which brings me to Janis Joplin, and ultimately to a

recent knife fight I had with a tube of ultramarine blue paint.

Janis Joplin was twenty-seven when she died in 1970, having had about five years in the hot weird limelight of the 1960's, boldly singing the blues for the stoned. She would be fifty-two years old this year if she had lived this long. She's been dead now almost as long as she was alive. She had a voice the size of a mountain, with the energy and power of a thunderstorm.

Her personal soundtrack and her music—the music millions of us heard—seemed to be pretty much the same. She sang at full tilt, get-it-while-you-can-*hard*, and then "right now" ended before anybody was quite ready for it. Her music was right on the money *about* her life.

I recently started several paintings. I made a drizzling mess of one, so in a fit I attacked it with a painting knife and a tube of blue paint.

It started to work into a pretty interesting piece, but ...

Time passed. Things sat.

One night, late, I decided to play every Janis Joplin tune we own.

I learned something.

This is what I learned:

"OoowOowoooOowoooOOoowoooh!" is a phonetic approximation of what ultramarine blue sounds like to me. And my painting needs more red, too.

What a beautiful set of colors she was.

▲ Power

Early one Saturday morning, I took a ride into Washington. It was before eight a.m. when I crossed the Potomac River and began riding down the Mall. There were already a lot of tourists, walking in the soft spring light. And on Constitution Avenue, the first motorcyclists of the day had begun to assemble, rumbling in on their bikes alone and in pairs, heaving them back against the curbstones at a slant and cutting their engines to wait until later in the day, when thousands more would arrive in the same way, "riding to the Wall," to celebrate Memorial Day. I was simply passing through, but I stopped to pay a brief visit.

It was a short walk to the Wall, as the Vietnam Veterans Memorial is known. I go there very infrequently. It's too powerful a place for me to go often.

Power, according to the dictionary, is "the ability to do, act, or produce." That is what the Wall has in its stark, silent simplicity, for me and many like me. It's awesome that way.

Initially, it appears like a surprise, a simple, subtle difference in the level of two grassy areas near the Lincoln Memorial, reminiscent to me of the rift I once saw in a garden after an earthquake. I followed a path down along this rift and watched my reflection glide down the black, polished wall set in its edge, until at the walk's lowest point my eyes were about six feet below the grassy rim at the top of the slabs. In about five minutes, walking slowly among a few men about my own age, some schoolchildren on tour, and a smattering of young couples, I passed by 58,000 names graven into the smooth black stone, names of people who died or were lost serving the United States in Vietnam between 1959 and 1975.

Here are some facts from the Wall:
- Jessie C. Alba's name is easternmost on the Wall.
- John H. Anderson, Jr.'s is the westernmost name.
- They both died on May 25, 1968.
- On a spring day, teenage kids look especially young against the Wall.
- Many of the names on the Wall belonged to kids.
- Jessie C. Alba was almost twenty-one when he died.
- John H. Anderson, Jr. was just twenty when he died.
- 1968 was a pretty bad year for young kids in Vietnam.
- The names on the Wall are almost impossible to read in a rain.

Power, the ability to do, act, or produce: Maya Lin, the young artist who designed the Wall, has it. The concept she came up with has it. The thousands of people each year who pass the Wall—all have the potential power to witness to each sad loss engraved in black granite there, and to the more personal dramas that play out daily between the lives enshrined there and the people who were parents and wives and husbands and sons and daughters and friends and comrades to those lives who come to visit.

The Wall itself is an interface with the power to transcend time and make a grief worthy of having available to us. And time itself has a most mysterious power—it enshrines the inevitable: change. At the Wall, a person can finally cut through the myriad wrenching changes that this country went through about the Vietnam debacle, and simply mourn the people whose lives we all lost in that most strange and terrifying time.

The first time I went to the Memorial, I carried my son on my shoulders through a quiet summer night. He was six or so. He was small and light, so far from being a man. He wasn't quite sure what the Wall was then. It was simply an occasion for a nice piggy-back ride in the dark.

I've been back twice since then. My son is a young man

now. That's pretty scary, so I go alone. I weep every time. The Wall is one powerful work of art.

I'd just finished working with a patient. I'd been working with her for several years in a therapy which moved as she moved, from grief to relief to hope, and in the end, briefly, back to grief as we said good-bye—but the good kind of grief, the sort that affirms that human life is worth grieving, the kind that acknowledges that living at its *best* involves relationships that, when their seasons are past, are mourned deeply in their passing as well as celebrated for their richness.

Art, like psychotherapy, is a movement through grief and loss to love, a transit from surviving to prevailing—creatively adding to the sum of the universe, rather than simply processing the status quo. William Faulkner, in his oft-quoted Nobel Prize acceptance speech in 1950, spoke of this, saying artists are privileged in their duty "to help man endure by lifting his heart, by reminding him of the courage and honor and hope and pride and compassion and pity and sacrifice which have been the glory of his past. The poet's voice need not merely be the record of man, it can be one ... of the pillars to help him endure and prevail."

Faulkner went further. He also wrote, "And who better to save man's humanity than the writer, the poet, the artist, since who should fear the loss of it more since the humanity of man is the artist's life blood."

Art abides in power. Art embodies power. Art empowers the creativity in each of us to emerge as we resonate to each other's work. All art is communication, and all communication is powerful in its potential to stir action.

My grandfather, an electrician by trade, once was almost electrocuted as a young man. At first, the only visible effect was that he lost most of his hair and what was left turned white. In his later years, he took up golf with a passion. He was a cautious player, except about one thing. When he got caught out in a thunderstorm, instead of ducking for cover, he'd calmly hold a metal golf club over his head and keep on walking in the open.

He never really explained why he did this to me. But it was a remarkable and terrifying thing to watch.

Sometimes power comes to us like a jolt of lightning, and sometimes it doesn't. As artists, though, we stand with creative golf clubs poised high over our heads, daring God to give us our due, in the name of our humanity, and that of our brothers and sisters.

▲ Doughnuts and Destiny

There I was, sitting in the local Dunkin' Donuts, reading Rainer Maria Rilke's *Letters on Cezanne*. It was early morning, my motorcycle was belly-up on a lift having its leaking innards attended to, and I was waiting, killing time and feeding myself with doughnuts and the literate ramblings of a man whose ability to get knee-walking giddy about art floors me.

Doughnuts—have you had experiences that serve almost like developmental icons, summoning up the full essence of critical periods of your life? You know, your first bike ride, first kiss, favorite teenage song, that sort of thing? Doughnut shops do that for me—they bring back the yearning, time-gnawing *ennui* and angsts of my early twenties, when a cup of coffee and time to stare wistfully at people in a doughnut shop was my greatest gift to myself. They served as way-stations to nourish me through the fatigue of waiting for love to come my way in a variety of wrong places; they gave me a place to soak up time like a young sponge immersed in an ocean, usually while waiting for a lover to appear so I could climb into her cloistering arms.

I grew to count on doughnuts to supply me with the epiphanies so necessary to youth. They were like communion before battle, and the shops were like smudgy chapels of the human spirit, where battered, dusted, twisted, half-baked, and hungry people of every town and locality came to tank up on the warm darkness of coffee and sweet pastry between hits at the world outside. They were open twenty-four hours a day, and so was I. It was a good fit.

I'm older now. After twenty years, I still know a good doughnut when I eat it, but I also know that it is likely to stay with me longer than I want it to.

Other things have changed too. I'm not quite so needy for angst that I spend much time looking for it anymore in doughnut shops and all-night diners. I need my sleep, and enough angst seems to find me during office hours that I feel plenty satisfied with my present supply. Moreover, cloistering arms aren't as desperately necessary for me these days. I'm not sure what to make of this fact, and there's a part of me that counts this change as a loss.

Lastly, I have begun to deal with the notion that I don't have a lot of absolutely surplus time left.

Rilke wrote to his wife, "Everything is yet to be done: everything." He was speaking of the feeling he believed he shared with Van Gogh that motivated the two of them to produce art.

I'm beginning to understand this motivation, I think, that overcomes the creative entropy even the best of us must contend with, this "no longer being able to postpone the work in view of all the many things that have to be done" in Rilke's words. It is the same energy, born of existential urgency, that drives pregnant women to clean before childbirth or that pushes estranged families toward reconciliation at the foot of a mother's deathbed. It is the energy that arises from the desire to create a change in the present, before the present ends, forever.

But there is another facet to creative motivation, a necessary presence, that actually makes a particular creative act "impossible" to postpone: it is the imperative involved that really releases the energy into action. I mean: what *must* be done, *will* be done. And either something must be done, because that is the inevitable way of things, or it can't be done.

Here is my take on a central organizing principle for the universe: from the first instant of creation, the movement through time of every particle of matter and energy has been a potentially predictable process.

In other words, the vicissitudes of faith aside, with a wide enough focus and enough understanding, chaos makes complete sense. And the future becomes predictable from the perspective of what humans, in their inevitable but limited genius, call "God."

Rilke had God as close to his mind as any artist when he wrote of an "infinitely responsive conscience." This is his take: "... how of one piece is everything we encounter, how related one thing is to the next ... all we have to do is to *be*, but simply, earnestly, the way the earth simply is ... not asking to rest upon anything other than the net of influences and forces in which the stars feel secure."

So much for philosophy.

We are a part of what is unfolding. And we, individually and collectively, will do each and every thing that must be done in this process. I believe this is the basis for the ultimate answer to what must be the most anxiety-laden question a working artist can be driven to ask: "What do I do to resolve blocks in my creativity?"

The answer is: "Anything. Everything. Nothing."

A lousy answer, no?

No.

If it is in you to produce, you will produce. You cannot do otherwise. If you do *anything*, it is possible you will do everything. The only way you can do nothing, is to *do* nothing. This is not complicated. It is not deep. It is a stone cold bean-counter's fact. Whether you act now or later, you will act if you must. Trust yourself. If the colliding particles and vibrations of your life shape you into a "doer of art," you will. In Rilke's words, "The time and composure and patience must ... be there ... the knowledge will be there ...."

If this seems like a notion that skates into the time-honored philosophical morass of pre-determination versus free will, I think it is because pre-determination is a concept used by theologians to describe in their own way what can also be described as "going with the flow." It is functionally impossible for human beings to be aware of all of the "flows" at work. Whether there exists a higher intelligence, a God if you will, who is able to grasp all the currents of the universe is beyond knowing, in the physical order, yet not necessarily beyond sensing.

But the fact is, we cannot know. So as far as humans are able to be aware, the future is up for grabs, each and every moment of it. Ta-dahh! Free will! Or what feels like it. Whether the next moment is inevitable or not, we don't know it. What we are about to do, or not do, feels like, and functionally *is*, up to us.

▲ CRITIQUE

At a party one night when I was younger and more soulful, I fell into a conversation with an English professor. He asked me what I did.

I said, "I'm a writer."

He asked, "What do you write?"

I replied, "Well, mostly it's in my head—I think about things to write."

Kindly, gently, patiently, he looked at me and said, "You know, you're not a writer until you *write*."

I believe that's the most helpful critique I have ever received.

The process of critique is familiar to most artists—the effort to derive understanding of the aesthetic success or failure of one's works by self-inspection of the work, or by its exposure to the critical responses of others like mentors, other artists, or the public at large.

A second process familiar to many of us is that of consciously drawing inspiration from our psychological perceptions, intuitions, and struggles. For many of us, personal experience and emotions are rich but often mysterious sources of our creative energy and subject matter. However, art critiques are often done without a specific focus on the person of the artist. The work stands alone, separated from its creator, in this kind of evaluation.

At least for some of us, though, a critical investigation which yields an increased consciousness of ourselves as well as our art could provide us both a deeper understanding of the art we produce, and a broader path to future production. The benefits of undertaking such a critique include the potential for enriching our art through an increased understanding of the sources of that art, developing awareness of personal symbolic languages, and providing a deeper, more accessible reservoir for new works. In a nutshell, it's how we can develop, as artists, and as humans.

The process of honest critique is "safe" in that it is unlikely to stifle creative ability or shrivel unconscious sources of creativity. I say this based on a view of the artist's unconscious, intuitive sense of self as essentially protective and competent to preserve his or her creativity from unwitting destruction. The Muse of Art is not as delicate as she is cracked up to be; she can reap from whatever field is available; and she is capable of taking care of herself.

This is not to say, however, that criticism wielded insensitively or incompetently—or worse, maliciously—does not have the same power as a spiked club to injure and stifle and thwart creative growth.

The moral here is to carefully pick your critics. Bad critics are worse than ignorant thugs. This also applies to yourself as your own critic. No one potentially knows us as well as ourselves, but most of us have enough blind spots, inbred prejudices about ourselves, and pockets of downright self-hate that we need, usually, to take what we think or say about our own work with a grain of salt.

Thus, it's real useful to have someone else you trust be a bit involved, whether as a guru or as a simple spectator, to keep things in balance. You could hire a guide, in the form of a professional critic, mentor, or therapist, or you could barter with fellow artists, providing each other with attentive feedback and respectful criticism.

Getting involved in an intensive critique is akin to the creative process itself. The risks involved are similar: potential failure to achieve the desired result; the potential for discomfort; the loss of illusions about ourselves and our work; the potential for blocking, avoiding, or unconsciously "missing the point" in our art and in our self-awareness. But for most artists, it is a process which for good or ill we cannot avoid because, in the end, it is an *integral* part of any serious effort to produce creatively. It behooves us to make it as useful a process as possible.

So, most of us do spend a large chunk of our creative time and energy simply thinking about and looking at our own work, deciding for ourselves what we've learned and what we have to offer in each piece we produce. Especially for those of us who consciously work with the idea that each work says something about us as artist, it helps to have some clear sense of our own emotional life histories—the significant patterns in our experiences and relationships, our beliefs, and so on—to refer to in exploring the meaning and aesthetic value of our artwork.

To this end, there are several tools that can help make sense of these things. These techniques were originally developed in order to study family processes and to be used in psychotherapy with families.

For instance, you might draw up a genogram—a symbolic, annotated representation of family information, kind of like a family tree, fleshed out with emotionally significant information about relationships and perceptions and attitudes contained in your family life. Monica McGoldrick's book *Genograms* is worth reading to gain an understanding of how to develop a genogram for yourself.

Especially useful is a time line of your life, including as many emotionally significant events as you can think of, from the day you were born until the present. You can make one by drawing a line on a long strip of paper—computer paper is perfect—and marking off the years between the beginning of the line (the time around your birth) and the present. Then, at appropriate places along the line, jot down brief descriptions of the significant events that occurred and memories you carry from your past.

Making up these graphic organizers of personal history

is an instructive process in itself, as most people find themselves thinking about connections and stimulating a lot of significant feelings which can become very useful in understanding themselves and their creative work. And once done, they provide a ready framework to juxtapose with one's creative work. New information often emerges in seeing clearly, for example, the historical context of the moment in one's life when a particular piece was created, and yields new learning about both the artist and the art.

Clive Barnes, a drama critic for *The New York Times*, once wrote, "I am convinced that anyone can be a great writer ... if he can only ... tell the naked truth about himself and other people. That, a little technique ... and the willingness to bare heart, soul and body are really all it takes. But few people know the truth, and fewer have the artistic intent and perhaps ruthlessness to tell it."

The process of learning the truth about oneself and one's art is often, as Barnes also wrote, "as hard as the nails on a crucifix." But it seems to be worth doing.

▲ Living Room

It used to be that the vast majority of people on earth lived and died without ever being more than fifty miles from their birthplaces. It probably still is that way for a majority of the earth's population. But for most Westerners, life today is very different. Typically, we change not just jobs, but careers, four times in the course of our work lives. Many of us travel fifty miles a day between home and work without a passing thought. And many of us could arrange, if necessary, to fly to the other side of the world by tomorrow morning.

As a result, an interesting fact, mostly true: we are freer, as a society, to change where we live than any humans have ever been.

But a lot of people seem to spend their lives living as if they aren't where they want to be. They feel like prisoners, bound to where they are out of a sense of duty, or tradition, or expedience, or need, waiting to be somehow freed.

Some of us aren't quite sure exactly where we want to be—we just know, or think, it's ... elsewhere.

I have this idea that an artist's studio is personal holy ground. It is the "... elsewhere" for an artist. In our studios, we create visions and movements, and sounds, and thoughts never before made real. And in so doing, we create and redeem our selves from the human state of displacement and occlusion that we share with most of our brothers and sisters, day to day. We do so by making our humanness known, and available to others to learn from. Pretty heady stuff.

Consider—as the place where thought and feeling become tangible, a studio often becomes a work of art in itself. What artist has not looked around his workplace every so often and felt pleasure at simply being there? How many artists throughout time have failed to resist the impulse to paint or draw their studios? Such images often become exquisite in their complexity as statements about the person, place, and process of the artist, his or her art, and art in general. They are a lot like images of mirrors reflecting mirrors—endlessly self-absorbed, endlessly suggestive.

I enjoy visiting artists in their studios. I know I am not alone in this, and I know why I like it so much. I like knowing people in-the-round. I like being where the action is. An artist's studio is a powerful self-portrait, and in many ways, the most intimate place on earth for that person. In the same vein, if I really want to be known by someone, I take them where I paint. For me, it's as intense a place as my bedroom (and my wife doesn't mind).

I also like to visit artists in their homes. For the artists whose work I really enjoy, it is remarkable how often their homes and their studios are at the same place. To me, it makes sense. If home is where the heart is, the studio is where the heart emerges. When both are the same place, there is likely to be an appealing congruence to what is produced there, whether it is artwork or children.

Sometimes we get lucky enough to stumble onto the obvious.

I work at a psychiatric center where children and adolescents live and go to school as part of their psychiatric treatment. Some stay a few months. Some stay as long as a couple of years.

After several years of having two active artists on staff, it finally dawned on us recently to get serious about arranging an "artists in residence" studio experience for some of the kids. In so doing we are aiming for something quite special with these kids: an opportunity for them to feel at home with the personal identity of "Artist" by working alongside adult artists as equals, in a real studio, with materials worthy of respect, and with the clear expectation that everyone involved is out to produce art, according to his or her own unique vision.

In the vernacular of the day, it doesn't take a rocket scientist to realize that art is a potent source of identity for some kids. Art is a means to discover and express the things that make an artist one-of-a-kind, the only possible creator of the work at hand. It is a process which demands commitment to action, and with the very first action taken, the doer has an identity: "Artist."

Moreover, the potential of art as a source of lifelong identity makes it one of the few activities available to kids which is equivalent in definitive power with the act of becoming a parent—an action which many kids undertake long before their times. There are many other things which similarly provide an identity-of sorts for young people in search of quick answers to who they are: drinking too much, being more reckless than the next guy, being prettier, or sexier. However, art is a lot less toxic, and has the advantage of not being "as-if adult" behavior: a six-year-old *can* be a *real* artist.

In our studio, we hope that by making it a place where creativity is the name of the game and by being creative ourselves, we can invite a few kids to find a home in their art, and reality in their identities as artists.

Identity is a tricky concept—it has to do with who we think we are, and who others think we are. It has to do with what we know about ourselves, and what we believe about ourselves. It has to do with learning to be authentic and unique in a world where dissemblance and conformity are often rewarded or required. It has to do with being willing to be intimately known by others, "transparently," as psychologist Sidney Jourard has phrased it.

For adolescents, whose primary task in life is to learn who they are, identity formation is what a lot of their behavior is about—answering questions such as: "Who's the boss, here?

What *do* I want? What can *I* do to get it?" One of the best things adults can do is help kids try on a variety of answers to these questions, safely. Another thing adults can do is to help kids experience what "really" being someone is all about. What this means in practice is for us to respect, in the same depth and sincerity as for other adults, the efforts our children make to define themselves as unique, to "be" who they are, even when it turns out to be different from what we think they should be.

It is often excruciatingly tough to do this, in practice. Respect for unique vision is not the same as permission to act irresponsibly, and adolescents are often exquisitely equipped to blur the distinction.

We all need living room. For some of us, this simply means we need the space and time to go through our lives without undue restriction and enough room to breathe. For some of us, however, child and adult, it means room to carve out our own view of life's meaning—the expression of which is life itself to us. We are artists.

▲ Foundations

Humans are relatively inefficient organisms. On average, we use around ten percent of our potential, according to many estimates. Yet, each of us is so outrageously potent that, given one day of maximum output from every member of the human race, the possibilities are almost unimaginable.

The "I" in each of us is the result of genetics, luck, and learning. We pass the world through filters of cognition, emotion, memory, and mood which are custom-built into our psyches from the minute of our conception, and tuned for the moment at hand until the hour of our death.

Each time we allow ourselves to respond to the world we are engaged in a creative process. As unique as snowflakes, we perceive and interpret reality in a highly idiosyncratic manner. Creativity occurs when we report these perceptions and interpretations to ourselves or to other human beings.

In a sense, creativity is simply life being communicated. Every conversation, scribble, and movement is a new creation in the universe, heretofore unseen and unheard throughout the ages.

There is another level of creativity accessed by some but not all—the realm of art and creative science. The price of entry: becoming as open (and thus vulnerable) as possible to the fullness of our experience, and being willing to describe it to others, as honestly and originally as possible.

Even in art, this natural law applies: we cannot create something from nothing. The unique reality each individual perceives is rare earth to be built upon and mined in search of new forms. In addition, we stand on our ancestors' shoulders. We exist today atop an ever-growing mountain of our forebears' experiences, of their unenacted ideas, concepts waiting to be connected, and visions waiting to be described.

Ultimately, we have only two choices: we can either sit atop the heaving mass and passively watch it grow, or we can reach in, grab the clay closest at hand, and expand the universe with our own creative work.

There are two deep, rich mines in this mountain of raw material: our conscious and unconscious experience as individuals and as a race. Moreover, the boundary ground between the two mines constantly shifts, and is far from barren itself. Artists and scientists play with the boundaries here, and dare enter the pits. We learn that the interfaces are where the action is. It is how we see colors that don't exist, yet. And hear music that doesn't fit on any staff, yet.

Consciousness, according to Freud, is our "instrument of psychic exploration." Our awareness provides us with access to the details of life itself, the patterns and interrelationships that ultimately form the tight weave of the universe. Our conscious imaginations serve as time machines at our immediate beck and call, and the past and future become our present. The minds of the weakest among us are still powerful enough to reach the end of the universe and return, within the beat of a heart. Any of us can select, arrange, visualize, and reconstrue whole scenes in the time it takes to put the dot on an "i." The artists among us distinguish themselves by using this power to guide the action that follows thought. The true limits are in our tools for action rather than our ability to imagine.

Consciousness provides us with the means to control our tools and shape our perceptions—to orient, prioritize, and select what we decide to enact. We can pick our pleasure for the moment, and tighten our focus on goals at the horizons of human experience.

What then of the unconscious realm? Does it even exist? What can it hold for us?

In simple fact, we are unconscious of the larger part of our human experience. In any given moment we attend, we can only attend to a small part of the universe that affects us. We can alter our conscious awareness, we can shift it and focus it, we can do almost anything but attend to *everything* that is going on. As an example, consider: when you concentrate on an itch at the end of your nose, you may be unaware of the beat of your heart and the rise and fall of your chest, and that the draft in the room chills you, the radio continues to play, and so on. But do these experiences not exist?

Our unconscious functioning is constantly nourished by information we don't realize we have, and operates free of the constraints of logic, criticism, and conscience that guide our conscious thought. Intuition, dreams, "aimless" action—these are pathways to our unconscious life. By allowing our conscious focus to relax, we can enter this tacit dimension of knowledge, described by Michael Polany, where ideas are "born of the imagination seeking discovery," where sentience itself emerges as a source of unreasoned truth. Here, opposites marry without censure and the full raw power of our feelings and fantasies marshals itself for expression.

Artists have been described by researchers as possessing thin, permeable psychological boundaries between themselves and the world about them. In fact, what makes artists unique among the race is twofold: their acute vulnerability to the awe of the world, and their ability to act in response to it. That creative work is produced by these individuals is a testament to the courage and focus required to be productive rather than frozen in the face of intense physical, mental, and emotional stimulation.

When I was a kid, I remember thinking that every thought I could possibly have had probably already been thought by someone else. How could *I* be creative? How could *I* be an artist?

Recently, I heard a friend explaining why he didn't concern himself much about others taking "his" ideas and using them. He had determined that, even armed with good ideas, very few people ever *enacted* them.

Somewhere in the world today there breathes a person capable of creating the equivalent of fire, given some time, and perhaps a cup of tea. Will this person act upon her thoughts? Will she press and mold her new visions into concrete reality?

Seen from afar, we must all look very similar. Shades of difference fade with distance, and the only thing that can be distinguished is who moves and who doesn't. The artists among us are the movers.

▲ Where's YOUR Studio?

It began when I invited my friend to go to a beer expo with me one Saturday. Then I suggested we swing by an open studio event I had been invited to, on the way. Art and brew—God lives in the details of life, and we were going to attend to a couple of very pleasant details here.

We arrived in due time at the Jackson Art Center, an old former public elementary school in the Georgetown section of Washington, D.C. In its present incarnation, the building provides studio space to a group of thirty artists whose work ranges from photography to metal sculpture.

First surprise: the food—the quality of the food. Within our first ten steps into the place, we hit chow. My friend quickly dragged a cracker through some salsa and pronounced it good, really good. By the time he did so I was deeply into the smoked turkey, myself. There was enough food for a convention of sumo wrestlers, and mind you, it was tasty, a good long step beyond skewered cheddar chunks and jug wine, good as that is.

In a while, with shards of meat atop a hunk of bread balanced on a plastic glass of red wine, I felt prepared for anything. Art! Open studios! Hubba, hubba!

I had been invited to the center by Ingrid Putschi, a woman who had helped me once at a frame store. Ingrid Putschi paints large oils, sensuous landscapes of the human figure, and makes tile-inlaid book covers. My first foray away from the food was to find her and say hello. Then, after we swung back through the cheese and meat and fruit, and refilled on wine, my friend and I began to look around.

Second surprise: the quality of the artwork. With a wide range of focus, technique, and style, the work was uniformly well-crafted. It was clear that these folks were serious about the doing of their art.

From Rebecca Abrams' beautiful photographs of women looking into our eyes as they alone wish, to Shoshanna Ahart's capturing the sense of place in her work, to Simma Liebman's layered paintings in evolution, to the meticulous abstract color work of Len Baron, there was common evidence of commitment to creative effort. And then there were Anne Waddell's landscapes, up against her constructed "instruments of celebration"—pay attention, her art is worth watching for, and her daydreams enacted in paint are both ethereal and faithful to the nature I know. I like her stuff.

Several of the artists in the Jackson Center are full-time pros. They make their livings at their easels or camera tripods. Others have kept their day jobs to float the studio rent. Whatever the case, the studios uniformly had a "sense of place," even rearranged to welcome and withstand the onslaught of an impressive mass of humanity as on this particular open studios day.

Some of the artists were clearly interested in the marketing opportunities the day offered. Others seemed more interested in relaxing with new friends, old friends, and whoever walked in through the door. And some, I think, opened the doors to their studios and went home for a while.

To each his or her own, and in so doing the day seemed to work well. I saw some red stickers up near works. My friend was recruited to do dray work on the spot for an artist in the thick of showing large rich landscapes to someone. We ate well, drank well, and experienced an intimate enjoyment that comes from being invited into the living spaces of living beings, people who on any other day of the year will be using their studios as shelters within which they can splash and sift and struggle, in privacy, with their chosen processes to produce new images and create pieces we cannot this year even conceive.

In a way, being invited into a person's studio is like being invited to go through his or her library, or medicine cabinet. You get to see an often edited but always substantial catalog of personal information about the artist and his or her creative process.

This fine old building, located as it is by Dumbarton Oaks, a site of political creativity in an earlier time in our history, is one of hundreds of places like it throughout city after city in our land—filled, with a waiting list, by creative people who want space to work, special space, apart from their homes, in a common place where they may or may not see the other artists around them for weeks or months of a given year. But they know they are there, behind their studio doors, doing the same soul-sweaty work as themselves—and that is what appeals about such a place.

Years ago, I spent a couple of years in a wreck of a studio building across from the National Portrait Gallery. For me at the time, it was like being in a powerhouse with a steady hum of energy in the air—a power enough to transform a firetrap into a creative center of the universe in my mind. We used to get our models by chatting up the dancers who took breaks in the park beneath our window from their jobs at the Gayety Burlesque House around the corner.

The Gayety Burlesque House no longer exists, and now I work at home. For many of us, working at home works best. It offers what we need to produce—the separation, the sense of aloneness that makes best for creative thought in some of us, at some point in our lives.

For some people, creativity in art benefits from a lack of distinction between art and living. For some, our creativity in art and our lives are bound so tightly together that our works are literally byproducts of the "performance art" that is our lives. My friend is like one of these artists in a sense. His "performance art" is the appreciation of people, and his ability to describe them. His creative product is a volume of work that would crush most of us, and his saving grace is an ability to fantasize about what could come next in life. He has worked for others, he has worked for himself, and he has learned what works for him, at least for the moment.

The advice here: find what you need to be creative—work with others, work alone—pick which works best for you—and *do* it.

We went on to the beer expo. We have decided what comes next in life. We are going to open a micro brewery in the Bahamas.

▲ Insight and Ignorance

I like Travis McGee novels, the ones by John D. MacDonald about the guy who lives in Florida on a houseboat.

The main character in these paperbacks has a pretty interesting attitude toward retirement, I think. He takes it now rather than later, a piece at a time, and works in between retirement periods to stash away enough to knock off again for a while.

I know, I know. How will he do so when he gets older, when he's no longer quick and tough and clever? Will he have enough saved up then to keep himself afloat in Boodles gin and the Bahia Mar Marina? Who will look after him as he gets older and stiffer and more senile?

That kind of thinking keeps most of us more steadily employed in our younger years, busily stuffing retirement accounts and arranging insurance plans in preparation for our "leisure years." But then, how many of us—well-insured and ready to collect on the industry that ate our youthful time—keel over shortly after we receive our gold watches and good wishes for the golden future?

The answer is, who knows? Real life is often nasty, brutish, and sometimes not short enough.

Here's some advice. Have the insight to see what the possibilities in your life are, and the ability to ignore the scary possibilities just enough. Pursue mightily the possibilities that attract you in your soul. As advice goes, this is as good and as easy to follow as the advice all good stock market players try to follow: "Buy low, sell high."

A second piece of advice: once you've thought a bit, *do* something. Do it sooner rather than later. Do it often. If then you don't like what you're doing, do something else ... and keep it up. Keep thinking. Keep doing. Then die happy.

Insight—this is one place where a Webster's dictionary definition ascends to the status of poetry—is, "the ability to see and understand clearly the inner nature of things." The goal of human thought is insight into our existence. The absurdity of the human condition is that we love to make this goal hard to reach. We do this by settling for partial glimpses at "the inner nature of things," and then calling these glimpses the Final Vision.

We do this so consistently that you would think any thinking person would recognize the scam immediately—but in every arena from science to religion to art, both history and today's newspapers are crammed full of evidence that in arguments about topics from cold fusion to the ordination of women to the value of photorealism, the kingdom of Man is a realm of folly in this way. As a species we tend to stop 'way too short in most of our inquiries into life, or get real cautious about potential changes in our "knowledge," far out of proportion to the risks involved in reforming our view of the world, kind of like the people on a superhighway who slow to ramp speed two miles before their exit.

As Robert Motherwell once observed, "It may be that the deep necessity of art is the examination of self deception." Insight is the meat of art. As artists, our lives are spent trying to get ourselves a clear vision of the inner nature of things, and trying to convey this vision to others in some way. With our creative brethren and sisters in science and philosophy, we are often in front of the crowd pushing through our own fears and doubts and yelling, "Hey, look! You've gotta see this!" But the crowd, surly and slow to stir, from its point of view sees only what seems like a gaggle of impulsive idiots making an inane and pointless rush toward mirages beyond the known horizon.

The vision of the Divine has traditionally been withheld from Man lest he perish in viewing it. As a race, we sense this risk, and those of us who are trying to peer past the veil risk the displeasure and at times the violent censure of our fellows as well as the anger of God at our hubris. And mark it, art is often full of hubris. Picasso put it this way: "There are painters who transform the sun into a yellow spot, but there are others who, thanks to their art and intelligence, transform a yellow spot into the sun."

Insight carries risks.

I have often daydreamed about what it would be like for me if one night, I opened the door to greet one of my daughter's dates and could know, beyond any doubt, that the youngster in front of me thought, felt, and behaved exactly as I did at his age.

I'd maim the kid—slam him right up against the front door a couple of times. Then I'd say hello pleasantly, and promise him more of the same if he so much as breathed heavily in my daughter's presence.

Sometimes insight is not a great blessing.

If I told you that I could arrange for a large mass of metal, say two tons' worth, with studs and glass and sharp edges all over it, to pass at a rate of 5,000 feet per minute within ten feet of you, and to do it again and again for say twenty minutes or an hour, would you leap to accept my offer? What if I further promised that there would be no external guidance for this speeding lump, and that I could almost guarantee that approximately one-third of the time, any internal guidance system in operation would be impaired and unable to operate at full capacity—what would you say then?

The obvious and only sane thing you would say is "No. No way. Not now. Not ever."

Let's put it differently. How about if I offered to drive you home tonight, and tonight happens to be Friday night in your town, wherever you may live?

No, insight is often what leads to phobia for many of us. For most of us, it is useful to be ignorant of some of the realities we contend with on a day-to-day basis. Driving a car is only one of these realities.

Enter the useful ability to maintain one's ignorance.

I frankly think Webster's incorrectly defines "ignorance," giving it only the meaning of *failing* to have knowledge or education or experience. Consider this the beginning volley in a crusade to recapture the useful aspect of being ignorant: ignorance is also the ability to be *oblivious* to information or past experience. The ability to ignore reality as we understand it is a tool we all need on occasion. But it is imperative for us to know that's what we're doing, and to do it selectively.

In this sense, the ability to select and attend to some things while ignoring others is synonymous with the ability to concentrate, a clearly adaptive and useful ability. But it is also important, if not vital to one's creative ability, to be able to ignore what is "known" in our culture and in essence to take the risk of reinventing the wheel, thus perhaps finding out that it really might work better as an oval rather than a circle.

So much of what we believe is truth is what we *think* we know. It is the ability to be beyond this belief that makes us creative, and is truly our greatest gift as humans. But it is our propensity to resist doing so which makes us truly stupid and keeps us mired in a vale of tears and foolishness that must make God stare in awe at times.

Once again, Picasso: "Art is a lie that makes us realize the truth." It is good for us to have insight into both the lie and the truth, and the ability to choose to ignore either at times.

▲ Coming Into Focus

Voices. "He's unfocused ... he jumps from one style to another ... his work seems unrelated ... it's not a 'body' of work, it's a clumping of pieces ..."

Welcome to my personal nightmare.

Throughout my creative life, I've gone through periods where I've found it hard to stay with one thing long enough to wring all the good out of it, as a soup cook might say. I'll get started on a particular theme or style of painting, for instance; then the next painting I do will be completely different. I'll feel like I'm zigging and zagging around, producing artworks that stand like orphans along a crooked road, born of the same father but bearing no family resemblance to each other.

I'm aware of a variety of motivations for this skipping around. One is what feels like boredom. It often washes over me just after I've begun a piece. It's like I'll sit there and see an idea waiting to come out of the paint in front of me, and then—I'll lose interest in continuing, as if the interesting part of the job is over, and the rest is scutwork.

Or I'll feel lazy, as if the actual painting of an idea is more like house painting than creative activity. Or impatient, frustrated with the time and care an idea might require to be expressed in paint, and unwilling to put out the effort.

Or, I'll be up to my ears in a piece and it will occur to me that I really don't know what I'm doing, either with the materials or the ideas involved, and I'll lose heart. The piece begins to look rough, amateurish, and inept to me ... I really should go to school on the technique ... I wish I could do watercolor ... I'm really a fraud ...

Or, I'll start looking over my shoulder. I'll start to think that my work won't catch on with anyone who ever sees it—it won't be accepted, it won't sell—maybe I should change it just a smidge ...

In a nutshell, the basic experience for me is, whatever I happen to be actually doing, I'd rather be doing something else. If I'm working representationally, I'll want to do an abstract next. If I'm working in acrylics, I'll envy effects someone else can get in tempera or oils or watercolor—anything but what I'm doing, or can do, at the moment.

In a way, It's like a panic reaction. And the result, the zigging and zagging, is often like a panicky man avoiding what he fears.

What's going on?

Looking beyond the boredom, the laziness, impatience, distraction, doubt, and jealousy, there's something else I can occasionally be aware of: I'm unprepared to comfortably deal with the images that are waiting to be born in my artwork—like vivid dreams, they are too close to me, too true. Their birth has all the ambiguity and ambivalence involved that attend the arrival of looming, disconcerting strangers who insist you know them well.

I'd often rather avoid these particular strangers if I can, for no clear reason. I'd be much happier if they were dressed in clown suits, or covered with flowers or flags. Then they'd be ... nice. And I would love the images that emerge from me artistically to be ... nice.

But—no luck.

Some of us are tuned squarely, like an old crystal radio, to one particular frequency in life, whether it is a unique point of view, a certain emotion, or a special set of circumstances. Some of us seem fated to a certain creative role in life, one we might never pick for ourselves. At times like these, it takes a special kind of creative courage to stick with a vision or direction which is unlovely, and which demands sacrifice by the artist of his or her personal comfort.

Essays on The Psychology of Creativity

Artists whose fate it is to create this art often struggle mightily with an acute awareness of how their vision demands so much of them beyond mere effort.

So ... what do I do? What so many of us do at similar points—I avoid the unpleasantness. I don't paint. Or I project my discomfort and fear onto audiences, other artists, critics—and paint fearfully and tentatively. Or I deny my discomfort and lie about why I'm not painting: no time, no energy, too many obligations, *et cetera*.

Or, occasionally, I suppress my fear, and press on, eventually engaging with images which I wish consciously didn't need to be born of me, but are my fate to paint, as it were.

There is a different kind of creative casting around that also occurs—the kind that results in new directions that are focused and purposeful, the movement that is the creation of a cohesive body of related work.

As artists, most of us crawl before we walk, whether we start at age two or forty. Some people arrive at a sense of themselves early in life, others later. Like children trying on a variety of guises, most of us need to try on a variety of artistic viewpoints, techniques, and expressions in order to discover our most honest identities and voices. In this way we eventually develop our unique artistic styles—and we do *create* them, they are not there from the beginning. Raw elements of style—talent, physical dexterity, a unique vision—may begin to distinguish our work from the very first. But the forces that stamp our art with relationship, as strongly as our genes stamp our children, take time to develop. We need patience with ourselves to tolerate the taking of our "own sweet time" in developing as artists, even while recognizing that time eventually runs out.

It takes courage to crawl. And to experiment. I'm ashamed to admit how long I've avoided learning to draw, or study oil painting, or watercolor, as a result of my unwillingness to be a beginner. Further, it takes courage to stick with processes that aren't easy or quick or guaranteed. Learning in art or music or science means commitment of time, attention, and energy in search of skills and awarenesses which might not bloom and grow in predictable ways.

It's easier to watch TV.

Moreover, it takes courage to make a commitment to do one thing at a time, when there are so many other, equally intriguing things to do. This in particular is a difficult thing for many of us, once we get on a roll. Sometimes, we have to choose to be faithful to the creative birth of a specific idea, even at the risk of losing a chance to attend the birth of an equally deserving image. It takes courage to live where you are, when necessary, instead of where you want to be.

The opposite side of this truth is equally important. It takes courage to move, when it is time to move on.

There is something to be said for the notion that learning to change is both possible and vital for most of us. It is largely an illusion, however, that learning to change makes change easier. Change is disconcerting by its very nature. It always involves loss of some sort. And in the midst of frequent changes, the losses tend to accumulate, while the gains tend to become harder to grasp. When it is time, however, the ability to tolerate the often powerful feelings associated with transition—fear, ambivalence, confusion—allow the gains to be made.

New perspectives and new visions are often available only to those of us willing to change our point of view when necessary. The price we pay is the discomfort of losing focus for a while. But, ultimately, the gain is that we may see even more clearly than before.

▲ CRITICAL INTERSECTIONS

Intersections of any kind are exciting places.
I was at a stoplight in the midst of an intersection—this one filled was with cars, trucks, and jaywalking Virginians—when the ideas for this essay first started to come together. I had, as part of the context of the moment, also recently been reading Stephen Hawking's *A Brief History of Time*, Jerome Stolnitz's *Aesthetics and Philosophy of Art Criticism*, and my nine-year-old daughter's latest short story. It was quite an intellectual brew.

Hawking, a theoretical physicist, recently wrote a bestseller which among other things allows mere mortals to grasp some of the most momentous and profound thinking yet available about the universe. Moreover, Hawking gives access to the implications which come from Newton's theories about gravity, Einstein's ideas about the relativity of time, and his own work in attempting to develop a unifying theory of physics to describe phenomena at both the universal and subatomic level.

There I was, sitting in traffic, thinking about how every clear night that I cared to go out and look up, I could see the universe as it was millions and millions of years ago. At any given moment on such nights, light which began its journey to earth eons ago is only just now arriving. I was in awe. We are seeing, in our daily night skies, the light of awesome cataclysms, the Armageddons of stars which have burned out before our world was even formed.

Think of it. Even our daily sunshine is eight minutes old. We constantly bask in the light of past events, our lives influenced by the convergence of past effect upon effect intersecting with our own personal "now."

If we allow ourselves to push further, we become aware of another intriguing concept. Rushing toward us, at the speed of light, is a past we will not encounter until the future. The universe's past does not exist for us yet. We have, in Hawking's terms, not yet entered its "light cone."

What about experiences that occur to each of us that are no less real, and no less momentous than the arrival of the light of stars? Imagine. At this moment, we are functionally unaware of the lives of the vast majority of our fellow inhabitants on this planet. Our "light cones" intersect only marginally. For all a farmer in the Hunan Province of China knows or cares, I might as well have lived in the fifth century B.C. Or be presently living on Neptune.

At this same moment in the expanding history of the universe, however, he and I are bound together as tightly as peas in a pod, brothers amongst millions of brothers and sisters, hurtling together on a very small world toward a future we have not yet intersected.

Here is the stuff of real wonder: how do our individual lives affect each other?

At this point in my reverie, my mind drifted toward the notion of criticism in art, a definite area of intersection between humans. It seems as if in the life of an active artist, there are two general states of being: being worried about producing, or being engaged in a critique process.

At its best, criticism by oneself or by others is the tool by which a creative person can bring himself, or be guided, to a state of uninhibited aesthetic productivity. However, the state of being purely active, confident enough in one's own voice or point of view to be free from conscious evaluation of the action, seems so elusive, so much a state of grace, that for many of us it doesn't exist as an experience. It is out of our "light cones."

In discussing aesthetic development, Jerome Stolnitz, a writer and professor of aesthetics, says there are two distinct purposes to criticism. One purpose is to clarify or explain the various aspects of a creative action: formal and structural qualities, symbolic significances, contextual implications, and so on. The other purpose is to evaluate the aesthetic worth of the activity, its "goodness" or "badness," effectiveness, validity, and value to an audience.

The creative process is an attempt to act in such a way that one's product is a unique expression of something important about life. To the extent that a product succeeds in being unique and, to apply Stolnitz's criterion for a valid critical interpretation to the art itself, "guide[s] ... attention, so that there is a difference in the felt quality of ... experience," that product is valuable.

To be able to achieve this creative end, it usually does not hurt, and often helps, to know a bit about what you're doing, and about what others have done before you as you work. This is where careful, skillful, informative criticism is invaluable.

Criticism may expand an audience's ability to appreciate a work or add layers of potential interpretive meaning to a piece and so enrich its aesthetic value. It may provide criteria by which work can be qualitatively evaluated.

But its most important function, in fact its only relevant function for the artist, is to inform him about what happens when his activity becomes concrete. Good clear thinking which draws forth the intrinsic aspects of the work itself, yet which can describe and extend understanding of the social, political, and psychological context in which the work was created and by which it was influenced, and which provides information to the artist of the personal impact of the piece on the critic—as useful feedback for an artist, what could be better?

If—and this is a big if—the result of criticism is more creative activity, and artists or would-be artists are expanded by it and freed by it to more confidently make unique statements, then criticism is useful. However, it is amazing how universal an experience for people bad criticism seems to be—bad in the sense that it is ill-formed, or careless, or ill-timed, or even ill-meant. Bad in the sense that, rather than stimulating creative effort, it smothers it, starves it, or thwarts it altogether.

Some of us will convert wonder at the universe into creative action. Some of us will stimulate that action in others, by our critical understanding of the creative process and of the work that results from it.

The intersection of critic and artist begins early for all of us. Our parents give us our first experience of critique. Subsequently, depending on the model they provide, we tend to experience criticism by others, particularly our instructors and teachers, as generally positive and helpful, or negative and limiting. Eventually, we internalize these experiences, and provide ourselves with an ongoing self-criticism that either helps or hinders us.

Be warned of your responsibility, parents and teachers of the world. Yours are professions which influence, often badly, the process of creativity itself. In future generations, along with prophets you will stand judged on the fruits of your present influence.

The light was going to turn green. We were about to move. Suddenly a phrase came to me:

"Some say they drowned. Others say they were eaten by pigs."

It was the last line of my daughter's most recent school assignment. I remembered how I felt as I looked up from the paper after reading the story. Part of me was floored by the surprise and enjoyment I got from the rhythm and impact of the words which closed her story about the misadventures of a couple of children sailing in the Pacific. Part of me was aghast at the horror borne in my baby daughter's mind. What would the teacher think? Was my daughter struggling with interior angst heretofore unrevealed? Was I a bad parent?

When, as gently as I could, I asked her how she'd come up with the ending, she explained, ingenuously I thought, that she didn't know how to end the story, but wanted to end it right then, so she came up with the pigs. It seemed to do the trick.

It made sense to me. And using Stolnitz's notions about criticism, she had come up with an elegant solution to a perennial creative problem. It's a rule in our house. The last sentence of anything has to have punch. Hers certainly did. Contextually, she had written the story to the required length of the assignment. It was time to finish. Her brother was deep into *Lord of the Flies*, and had not been shy about discussing the gorier points of its central symbolism during the previous few days. Her intention was to tell a story and get the heck done, so she did, using what she had available in a unique way. And intrinsically, her piece had drama, scope, and reflected the ironic ambiguities not only of a nine-year-old mind at work, but also of life itself. As art, it worked. I think. And so I told her.

If she writes another story, I will feel like a pretty good critic.

▲ Wrangling with Jung

Sigmund Freud conceived of art as the sublimated demonstration of an artist's internal conflicts, but in his writings seemed aware that there was more involved than that. The realm of art seemed perhaps the most difficult facet of human psychological life for Freud, in all his creative capacity, to elucidate. I like him for that.

Carl Jung, one of Freud's contemporaries, saw art as the concrete expression of man's collective psyche. In Jung's view artists were especially endowed with sensitivity to this unconscious pool of symbols and universal significance, paying for it in the loss of energy to develop and resolve their own maturity as individual human beings. I'm comfortable with his view of "art" (it gibes with my own), and I have heartburn with his view of "the artist" and his or her role in art.

These are some of Jung's ideas, published in *Modern Man In Search of a Soul.*

> What is essential in a work of art is that it should rise far above the realm of personal life and speak from the spirit and heart of the poet as man to the spirit and heart of mankind.

So far, so good. Most artists I know would buy that notion.

> The personal aspect is a limitation—and even a sin in the realm of art. When a form of "art" is primarily personal it deserves to be treated as if it were a neurosis.

To the extent that art that speaks only to the artist is

limited, I also accept this observation as accurate in my own work. At one point in my life, I was trained as and worked as an "art therapist." I grew uncomfortable with that identification, at least partly because to me it felt like much of the time, the artwork involved was more accurately termed graphic acting-out, and on other occasions, true works of art were devalued in the priorities of the artist's need for therapy. It was as if we were using the mechanics of art in a way rudely, with a lack of accuracy. I believe my discomfort with art therapy was mostly personal identity crisis at the time, but it does seem as though Jung's views help me now to understand what some of it was about.

He goes even further.

> There may be some validity in the idea held by the Freudian school that artists without exception are narcissistic—by which is meant that they are undeveloped persons with infantile and auto-erotic traits.

Here, we are getting a bit broad in our brush strokes, to my way of thinking. Even so, most artists, indeed most people I know, have some degree of focus on themselves, and some capacity for making themselves feel good. And to some extent, none of us is fully formed. Some of us are just a tad more aware of our lack of completion than others.

> The statement is only valid, however, for the artist as a person, and has nothing to do with the man as an artist. In his capacity of artist he is neither auto-erotic, nor hetero-erotic, nor erotic in any sense. He is objective and impersonal—even inhuman—for as an artist he is his work, and not a human being.

Interesting point of view. Insofar as I understand what Jung is saying, one becomes an "artist" by doing "art." To the extent that "art" speaks of man/womankind beyond just one person's experience, it is impersonal; but "inhuman?" Nahhh. Art is human. It can't be otherwise.

> Art is a kind of innate drive that seizes a human being and makes him its instrument. The artist is not a person endowed with free will who seeks his own ends, but one who allows art to realize its purposes through him. As a human being he may have moods and a will and personal aims, but as an artist he is "man" in a higher sense—he is "collective man"—one who carries and shapes the unconscious psychic life of mankind.

Once an artist becomes worthy of the title, i.e. does something to express the "collective psyche" in imaginative fashion, according to Jung, he or she becomes impersonal, a kind of lightning rod for the soul of mankind. He or she is taken over by the process of creativity, and becomes a conduit for symbols and meanings from the deep pool of largely unconscious common human experience. Moreover, he or she adds to the symbols and meanings in the pool, and in so doing, helps expand the depths from which subsequent generations of art and artists will draw. Not a bad job if you can get it. Kinda godly, in a way.

But there's a catch, according to Jung. You see, human beings have only so much energy in a lifetime. So you gotta make a choice, it turns out.

> To perform this difficult office it is sometimes necessary for [the artist] to sacrifice happiness and everything that makes life worth living for the ordinary human being .... The artist's life cannot be otherwise than full of conflicts, for two forces are at war within him—on the one hand the common human longing for happiness,

> satisfaction, and security in life, and on the other a ruthless passion for creation which may go so far as to override every personal desire.

Whoa, wait just a minute. Not true for everyone who does art. True for some, but it often seems more a function of society's low valuation of art as a profession and external difficulties in arranging for time to do art, or the support and care that can help. But Jung begins to sound like the price of the admission ticket to the realm of the artist is loss, rather than action.

> The lives of artists are as a rule so highly unsatisfactory—not to say tragic—because of their inferiority on the human and personal side, and not because of a sinister dispensation. There are hardly any exceptions to the rule that a person must pay dearly for the divine gift of the creative fire.

We seem to have a kind of chicken/egg debate cooking here. Are artists narcissistic and undeveloped because they sacrifice all to be creative, or are they creative because in their narcissism and rawness, they have access to the pool of mankind's common passions, and are driven to create by selfish need?

A final point, which seems a semantic one. Jung asserts:

> The secret of artistic creation and of the effectiveness of art is to be found in a return ... to that level of experience at which it is man who lives, and not the individual, and at which the weal or woe of the single human being does not count but only human existence. This is why every great work of art is objective and impersonal, but none the less profoundly moves us each and all.

Bruce M. Holly

Is great art "impersonal," or is it universally personal? I have an answer, for myself. No work of art that stirs me can fail to tell me about the artist who made it. I do not believe in "mankind" as an entity. I believe in men and women and children whose lives are intertwined infinitely across time, with common experiences and feelings and thoughts uniquely filtered by each individual life. We are all potential artists, working off the same palette, working on the same canvas. Some of us are wounded, some are whole.

▲ Point of View

As I write this, I sit surrounded by a most beautiful salt marsh, on a bright, cool morning during one time of year (early spring) when the humid, fly-bitten, swamp-reeking reality of a Chesapeake Bay salt marsh doesn't at least equal the beauty. There is a high south wind roaring up the bay this morning. It has pushed much of the water out of the creek, and brown tidal flats rim the purple and ochre expanses of grass and low brush around me.

This is my theory: salt marshes are where God sends artists to learn about line and subtle, gorgeous earth tones. To study white, He sends us to British Columbia in winter, and for dramatic, sad, powerful apprenticeships to the color gray, He gives us passage to either the high granite mountain ranges of the world, or to the lonely reaches of winter seas.

This is a debatable theory. Chroniclers of city life will, and should, insist that there is no richer instruction in the tones and shades of color than the bricks and stones and concrete their front stoops can offer. Insistent voices will counter them in declaring the human body, any human body, is the ultimate source of learning about the simple components of human art.

And in the end, we will agree that it doesn't matter a hoot what's in front of us, so long as we have our own particular minds to work with. Give us a sow's ear, and some of us will make silk purses, while some of us would open a vein rather than do anything but frame the ear and title it "Aunt Maudie."

We each have our own unique point of view. No matter how desperately we wish this were not so—and the study of human political history is the study of this desperation—this is an inalienable fact. We are stuck with uniqueness—condemned by the same random chaos that creates individual snowflakes to points of view that we can fully share with no other person ever to live on earth.

Each of us is a universe of one in this regard: we are alone in eternity in our personal experience of life.

Welcome to existential loneliness of the first order.

Now, then—so what? For a start—you alone are the author of your particular story. You really, really *are* the captain of your own ship. You have been handed your destiny, in the sense that you live where you live, you get what you get from your parents, from your environment, from your own resources whatever they are, and so on. But how you perceive that destiny, how you respond to it, how you document that response—are, in the end, in your hands, eyes, and mind.

Yours alone.

Wow.

I have a number of favorite places in this world. I will have more before I call it quits. That is for me a very comforting and intriguing thought.

At one time, I thought of my home town as a place of drudgery—a dank, dirty paper mill town in a valley drained by a polluted, scum-covered river in northern New Hampshire. Soot flecked the polluted snow of seemingly endless winters; my relatives died off one by one, of various cancers. I promised myself that when the last of the kin I cared about was in the ground, the town would become for me a forgotten place, a place I was from, not of.

Years passed. I left and returned with new eyes. I saw a place I'd missed before, a city of people for whom the valley *was* home—a home worth cleaning up, and preserving, and passing on to their kids with sense of pride. And above the town, in a way I'd not appreciated before, were mountains of a power and dignity I'd scarcely noticed for years.

More years passed, and I had children, a son and a daughter.

As he grew, my son took on a vision of the mountains I'd begun to claim, and took it further.

I led him into them at first, with him hopping and darting up and over the hard places with the erratic energy of puppy youth while I plodded with carefully husbanded strength in a steady gait I'd spent years learning.

I gave him a taste of the edge of things—we climbed together, roped, and he looked into a chasm from a pinnacle I'd discovered alone years before. I saw, watching him at that moment, how different we were, and how thankful I was for the difference, and how much the sight of him alive in my life meant to me.

Time passed, and he began to find his own high places, and sometimes now he'll show them to me from afar, and sometimes he'll take me back to them himself. I feel honored at those moments.

And some of those places can only be his alone.

In a different way, the same is true for my daughter, who seems to me a much more private person than my son, a young woman with a view of the world much different from mine, with interests I can only guess at. In her own time she occasionally invites me in for a look at the mind and imagination she keeps politely to herself. She has a confidence and toughness I would have envied as a kid, and a reserved style that seems at times so difficult for me to accept that it probably is similar to my own way of handling things.

She has her own favorite places and they're mostly close to home. Through her right now I'm learning about loving from a certain distance, and loving a young one for whom "home" has a meaning, a constant sense of favored place, so different from my own roving childhood that it is hard for me to fathom.

Back to the salt marsh. When we are there together, my son sees only a tableland of flats and water, devoid of the hard, steep places he's learning to love so well. My daughter has eyes only for the young children she loves to mother on visits to our friends who live amid the sawgrass and seabrush and salt wind. My wife, with a biologist's eye, sees the signs of life, the birthing, dying and eating of each other that animals do around us at every turn.

I see a landscape brimming with subtle feelings that stay just barely beyond my conscious reach.

▲ Apertures, Filters, and Fields

Human beings come factory-equipped with five senses, a brain, and (some say) a soul. With these tools, we construct our personal understanding of the universe, and add our perceptions and experiences to the pool of history. When our tools wear out, we disappear except in memory and in the concrete work we leave behind.

In a way, our tools for perception are similar to the mechanisms of a camera, auto-driven, constantly clicking away. The workings of our minds as we make something of our perceptions correspond to the darkroom efforts of a tireless but sometimes confused photographer, unsure of his aims, working on frame after frame of ever-incoming film, recognizing on occasion the subjects being imaged, but often out of touch with their meanings. The images thus produced are so varied in composition, content, and quality that our life's creative work is similar to that of a photo editor, culling the exquisite from the mundane, deciding how to frame it, and whether, where, and when to publish it.

For each of us, life enters our awareness through sensory apertures which are amazingly similar from person to person. Yet each is subtly unique. Our senses admit the raw data of life, light, heat, and uncensored feeling to our minds, where images are apprehended, developed, and cataloged. In our individual catalogs, each of us has similar basic experiences, beginning before birth.

We see and feel the same sun rising and setting, and thus become accustomed to a similar daily rhythm. Rich and poor, we all learn to honor our bread. We all hear wind and the crash of thunder, and learn to become intrigued by storms or terrified of them. Our common experiences and basic similarity with each other allow for a common language in communicating about life.

Our individual sensory differences, however, color and tune each and every experience. Thus, in truth, no experience is the same for any two people. Even when we listen intently to the same drummer, we all march to different drumbeats. At the same time, however, if we choose to, we can march in step with each other.

As we grow, most of us add filters through which life must pass before we process it internally. These filters are usually unwittingly constructed, and usually serve protective functions. Consciously, we believe that these filters, like the filters on a camera, serve to heighten our perceptions, increase contrasts, and ultimately clarify things.

Like all filters, however, they unavoidably diminish the potential power of that which they screen. Their usefulness is usually very specific, and our ability to consciously control their influence is often very limited. Some, like the ability to concentrate, allow us to focus in a world where in the quietest corner, a thousand things are always happening. Others, like racial prejudice, allow us to protect our personal inadequacies and misconceptions at the cost of human dignity.

To continue the analogy with photography, the fields of our experience are very influential. Like a camera, what we are exposed to is what we use to form our understanding of the world and to form the specific language with which we can respond to it.

When one is born in a pulp mill town in rural New Hampshire, one's images of the world begin with the vertical shadows of mountains and smoke stacks, the pungent scent of wet wood pulp, and the feel of factory cinders in air-dried clothing. With no other experience, it is entirely possible to write a story, or paint a picture, or compose music which describes human passion, joy, pain, and sorrow which someone from driest, flattest Saudi Arabia could comprehend. However, it would be unlikely that the New Hampshireman in question could convincingly use images of the desert he has never seen or felt or smelled, but with which the Bedouin in his audience is intimately familiar. For the most part, we use best that which we know best. And we know life best by being exposed to it as directly as possible.

Further, our ability to take in the material in front of us varies, much like a camera with various lenses. With a wide-angle lens, one can include a great deal of a scene and its many aspects, and convey much about the context in which the image is found. With a telephoto lens, one can see into distance clearly and apprehend detail, at the expense of context. Similarly, many of us see the forest much more clearly than the trees, while others of us can exquisitely describe the intricate molding of the bark on a single tree's branch, unaware of the forest burning around it.

In a recent book which captures this variety of field and focus in human creativity (*Uncommon Genius*, Viking Press, 1990), author Denise Shekerjian uses interviews of recipients of the MacArthur award, a no-strings financial grant given to outstanding people in a variety of fields, to explore the workings of creative minds.

Out of these talks with artists, playwrights, scientists, community organizers, and many others, several common themes emerged. As Shekerjian describes it, the creative among us commit themselves to using their talent, refining it as they go, sticking with it over a long haul. They accept risk in the pursuit of a personal vision, and learn to stay loose, often delaying resolution of problems until various possibilities and perspectives are explored. In general, they seem able to connect ideas in unusual ways, to see the linkages between disparate ideas, in much the same way as a creative photographer sees common scenes uniquely.

As individuals, these creative people tend to deliberately set up conditions that foster creativity in themselves. Some seek noise and bustle around them, others seek quiet. Some need the smell of ripe apples nearby, some need plenty of coffee. As a group, they are aware of, and prepared to deal with, the realities of the environment and times surrounding them. While they do not necessarily make pictures typical of the culture around them, they do work at learning how to get their work published and seen by others.

Above all, they value the doing of their talent above the preparing to do it. They clean and calibrate their tools, their apertures and lenses, as they go. They are aware of the filters they use and give thought to which are helpful and which need to be removed. They tend to work assiduously and deliberately at widening the fields of their experience through travel, study, and contemplation.

Shekerjian further notes that these folks tend to be pattern-seers and reframers of accepted perceptions. Many of them habitually twist and turn every idea and statement of accepted reality, like a photographer moving around a subject, until they can see things from new perspectives, before making any effort at closure.

In discussing what seems to foster creativity in these individuals, it seems we can define what limits it in others. We can also learn what happens in the interface between these folks.

The risks of creativity are intimately familiar to most of us. By definition doing new things means confronting ourselves, and those around us, with being unsettled, unresolved, and uncomfortable. At some point, we all struggle with a reflexive desire in ourselves and others to keep life familiar, to keep it understandable in light of what we already "know." Interestingly, the conflicts engendered by these pressures and constraints can make for strange bedfellows, and alternatively, place people with similar values about life at loggerheads as to the expression of their individual visions.

It seems useful at these junctures to remember that a variety of solutions are likely to exist for any human problem, if we keep ourselves open to their existence and to each other. Narrow apertures, heavy filters, and limited fields of view—when not used carefully and consciously—can make for meager, dark, and underexposed ideas, in photography and in life.

▲ CHOICES

We are born, we make choices, and then we die. We play with the cards we are dealt, but we largely choose how to play our hands and what stakes we will play for. We decide whether we will play our cards straight or whether we will bluff. We determine how we will see our fellow card players—as friends involved in the same game or as opponents to be feared or defeated at all costs. And ultimately, we alone decide if we have won or lost the game.

The same holds for art and artists. At every turn, art is a process of making choices. We as artists are decision-makers by definition, choosing to create—that is, to do something new in the world, and to keep at it until we decide our work is done. And then we choose if, when, and how we share it with others.

What then are some of the aspects of choice?

Ambiguity is the hallmark of an "adult" problem. As we mature, choices tend to become more complicated and less clear-cut. We become more aware of subtleties, variables, and alternatives; we have more information, advice, and experience to draw from. But we can easily draw contradictory conclusions from this knowledge.

Moreover, alternatives often include their own opposites. We are exposed to these notions daily, from the crass to the sublime: "You have to spend money to make money" ... "Every cloud has a silver lining" ... "We make our own luck" ... "They gave their lives so others might live" ... Most human choices involve "either/and ...," "either/or ...," or "all of these/and ..." or "neither/none of these" situations. Absolutes are very hard to come by, and emerge only out of acts of faith.

As we grow, the decisions we make usually have increasingly important, often far-reaching consequences. These decisions often involve others and usually involve pain as often as they involve gain.

And because life is fluid, far fewer choices are final than we believe at the time. Failure, like success, is fleeting. So too are the decisions we make that lead us to failure or success. We can, we do, we must change our decisions as life goes on. Even the most rigid and stubborn among us do so because nothing in our existence stays the same from minute to minute.

Do these notions apply to art and the creative process?

Human experience is a multilevel affair. So with art. Choices never have one level. Our experience is made complex because of our conscious and unconscious natures and because of our ability to think—that is, to step out of ourselves and contemplate our condition. We do this at every turn, in every second of our existence. What for an animal is a straightforward decision, i.e. "Do I eat this?" is for us, inexorably, a moment of moral significance in each and every instance—and in the end, this is the central difference between Jackson Pollock and an ape.

Consider the clichéd notion of art as a metaphor for human life. It is a cliché precisely because it is so valid. Art is the result of a decision-making process which yields creative action. Art is a fluid entity with boundaries and parameters that change through time, yet it is an entity which also transcends time. And finally, art is fraught with ambiguity, many levels of meaning, and risk.

Consider the characteristics of artistic choice. The immature artist acts as if choice were simple—an illusion brought on by ignorance and lack of experience, to be sure, but useful in allowing action to take place—and creates expressive but crude and limited work. We expect no more from the neophyte, and are awed by the occasional youngster whose work is technically or expressively beyond expectation.

With experience and growing maturity, the committed artist evolves a personal style, language, and expressive facility. This in turn yields a body of work which is evocative and informed by the artist's ability to deal with the ambiguity, subtlety, and limitations of his subjects, materials, and processes. His choices are no longer perceived as simple, whether they are made in an intuitive, impulsive style, or in a more deliberate, thoughtful, perhaps "scientific" manner. Complexity and ambiguity, and the artist's unique treatment of their existence, become an essential part of every artwork's impact.

What personal characteristics influence our artistic choices? There are many. For instance, some of us are "right brain" people: intuitive, illogical, impulsive. Our decisions are made often without our being fully conscious of the process we use to make them, and we are hard-pressed to describe the variables we consider in making them. On the other hand, some of us are "left brain" thinkers: deliberative, and demanding of ourselves that each choice be based on consciously considered, pragmatically evaluated, and solidly logical reasons. While one type is more likely to be an "action" painter, the other may more easily embrace pointillism. One artist will plow into thick impastos of images and textures that document changing thoughts and feelings of fleeting moments caught on the run; another consults color studies and tries color combinations on scraps before committing to a new hue in a pointillist painting which is years in the making.

Further, there are those of us who tend to see life as a glass which is half-empty, and who characteristically feel on guard against potential threats. Our art will likely express this stance in many ways: in subject matter, directness of expression, and mood. On the other hand, those of us who optimistically see the glass half-full, functioning as if the world were a safe, warm, and friendly place to live, will similarly demonstrate this frame of mind in our artistic choices. There are many exceptions here, however. A depressed artist may paint bright bowls of flowers in an attempt to transcend his black mood, and a well-adjusted, materially secure artist may create pictures of surpassing anguish and horror, perhaps out of a need to identify with other less fortunate humans, perhaps out of a sense of relief at feeling different, or perhaps out of unconscious personal pain.

Some people are inclined, given a choice, to explore the rare, the new, the frontiers of experience. Others prefer to study the known and familiar objects of everyday life from unique personal perspectives. Some of us prefer to declare our visions—others are more comfortable suggesting them. Taking the offensive comes easily to some, while others prefer to defend.

Within a wide range, these characteristics define our unique approaches to living and give us as individuals the eccentricity that makes life interesting. At their extremes, however, these "styles" of living and the choices they engender can be pathological in that they hamper life severely. In psychiatric terms, these are people with personality disorders—people who are paranoid, avoidant, hysterical, obsessive-compulsive, narcissistic, and so on. For these folks readjustment often includes intensive therapy and self-exploration over a long period.

In art, similarly, our styles of aesthetic decision-making can serve us well in defining our uniqueness, so long as we can be productive. It is when we find ourselves restricted or unable to move artistically over a long term that we need to consider the fundamental changes that may be necessary in order to return to productivity. It is here that the commitment to art and the commitment to life often overlap significantly, for change is not easy in this area.

For some of us, the risk of choosing and failing in life and in art is a loss of self-esteem which outweighs the potential satisfaction of success so completely that we are locked into immobility by fear. It is this that causes creative death far more frequently than heart disease. There is a quiet courage demanded of all of us with each breath we take. In art, this courage is manifested each time we choose to move toward a new creation.

To be artists, we must decide to accept ourselves as we are at the moment, with faith that we can confront the problem at hand and that we can repeat the confrontation over and over again until we have reached a creative end. What helps is being able to give ourselves permission to try, permission to have accidents, and permission to build on the work of others.

In the end, it is our full relationship with ourselves and others in the world, and what we choose to use of it, that is our real palette.

▲ A Sense of Place

All the world is a stage, and every inch has had countless dramas enacted upon it. When I was younger, I had a real conviction that this is so. I would, of an evening, go wandering until I came to some unremarkable spot. I would stop, and then—just wait.

Soon enough, one of two things usually happened.

Something interesting would happen right as I waited, ranging from cops stopping to ask why I was just standing, to a particularly beautiful cloud passing overhead, to someone passing by whose presence became to me magical, arresting, and without precedence. I began to count on this as a sure thing, and in my experience it was so.

Or, if things were just right, something else would happen. As I stood, a kind of trance would absorb me and I would become viscerally aware of the history of the place at which I stood, of the tragedies and comedies, passions and terrors that had in past moments throughout time occupied the place in front of me. As a result, I spent much of my youth in fascinated awe, a condition all young people deserve to experience as often as possible, as I think back now on my own experience.

And so, I wish this for you, here: do anything and everything in your power to encourage fascinated awe in yourself and especially, in your children. It is *always* a worthwhile thing to do, in my opinion.

Lightning struck a towering poplar tree just outside our daughter's bedroom window recently. A crashing flash of light, a red ball of darting fire, splintered shards of bark and wood blown yards away, broken limbs and streaks of bleeding sap. The big noble tree stood shivering in the aftermath, according to my wife.

Power, the ability to do—for ill or good—is everywhere. All the earth is power; all that surrounds us in life is power. Even time, the very ether of eternity, has a most mysterious power as it enshrines the inevitable, yet is the medium of change.

We humans live in a constant cosmic hum of energy. The diamond force of our wills to be, simply to be—that is *our* power. And the artists among us are those of us tasked, in William Faulkner's words, with documenting man's not merely surviving but *prevailing* in this environment. In the doing of our creative work, our potency is transformed into acts of love for the universe, whether we intend them so or not.

A few weeks ago, my wife and I drove through southern Maryland to Point Lookout, where the Potomac River meets the Chesapeake Bay. She needed to scope out the place for a school field trip. I was along for the drive in our new "midlife crisis" vehicle, a little roadster with room only for two friendly people and a couple of small toothbrushes.

Point Lookout looks out over some of the rougher water in the Chesapeake, being a point of confluence of winds and strong currents that often make for tricky sailing. It is a place of subtle beauty, especially on a calm sunlit day—a place of marshes and lapping water, scrub trees, and poison ivy; alive with ducks and osprey, egrets and fiddler crabs.

And it is a place of history, as all places are.

In 1864, Point Lookout became the site of a prison camp for Confederate soldiers. I remembered this when my wife noticed a tall obelisk in trees off the road to the point, marking a Confederate cemetery.

It became the largest prison camp of the Civil War. Three thousand, five hundred men out of 54,000 souls who passed through the camp before the war's end died in squalor and misery, cold, hungry, and debased by their countrymen. We had a concentration camp ninety miles, my friends, from our nation's capital, on one of the prettiest and most poignant strands of sand I've ever seen.

Today the sand where these men suffered is being eaten away by the Bay. Where many of them a few years back shivered and limped their way to either survival or death, water now covers the sandy site of their shacks and tents.

The ambiguous presence of Point Lookout—physically here today, gone (at least a bit of it) tomorrow—is fitting. Many such places, from Dachau to the killing fields of Cambodia, and more recently Rwanda, in another moment might well be called beautiful. But not by those whose knowledge of their human history is such that they cannot allow themselves the relief of innocent ignorance, whose experience of the place is too directly tied to the horror of a particular moment, a particular time.

In the end, though, we do regain innocence of a sort, a relief brought on by time, emotional distance, and unawareness—the blessed ignorance that gets humans through an otherwise overwhelming reality.

And the earth reclaims itself. It is as if nature cleanses itself of the moral stain of man's insipid cruelties toward his kind. But in fact, nature is indifferent to man, and we alone bestow the universe with meaning significant only to ourselves.

The ambivalent reality of Point Lookout is subtle and gorgeous. It is a place filled with life. Yet at any moment scared and angry men could easily die here in droves as they did in the 1860's; and the men who put them here could, without noticing it, easily find their own moral limits eroding like the sandy water's edge around them.

My wife is a teacher. Point Lookout is a wonderful place, it turns out, to teach people about a myriad of natural things. Birds fly over, much as I imagine they did on a day a hundred and thirty years ago, when tens of thousands of men camped here in fear and anger. Fish swim, crabs crawl, grass waves.

Yet even in the steady wind that blows across the water, there is an awesome silence to the place. It is a place of powerful currents that run through our time as surely as they did a century and more ago. But these currents, like the subtlety of beauty, are easy to miss; today at Point Lookout the reality of the place is kept alive by remembrance alone.

▲ Passion

It was early in the morning on Mother's Day. I'd just finished putting a coat of paint on the hull of my boat. I had it all figured out: this article would be about passion.

But first, let's talk about avoidance.

You see, I really should have had this article to the publisher four days earlier. But I'd gotten into the habit of stretching the deadline until it almost pops, and this month was no exception. Plus, the weather had been outrageously gorgeous, and my boat needed painting—but more about my boat later.

I came in, turned on the computer, and wrote out the first sentence of this thing. Then, I figured it was still early, so I decided to go get a cup of coffee. But it might be a while—so I decided to turn the computer off. It's better for the screen or something, I understand.

On the way to the kitchen, I decided to look up "obsessive-compulsive disorder" in my diagnostic manual so when I got ready to write about passion and how we all ought to have something that absorbs us and focuses our attentions, and creates "intense emotion" for us, like the dictionary says, I would be able to write about how being passionate is different from being obsessed, in a clinical sense, with unwanted, intrusive thoughts that often spark driven, repetitive, and sometimes harmful behaviors known as compulsions.

While I was rummaging for the manual, I ran into Rollo May's *Man's Search For Himself.* I hadn't read the book yet, but I wondered if Dr. May had anything to say about passion. So I went through the table of contents and the index. May wrote about loneliness, "hollow people," loss of values and self, loss of communication and ownership of life, the "struggle to be," and a most wonderful phrase: "Courage, the virtue of maturity"—but nothing specifically about passion that jumped out at me. I'd have to read it carefully, sometime. I put it on the floor in front of the bookcase. I'd be sure to notice it there.

I looked around the room. I'd wanted to say something in this article that referred to a biography of Jackson Pollock I'd been reading—the book was filed neatly on the floor behind my chair, so I would find it easily. Now, Pollock—there's a fella with a tough inner life, and an evident amount of passion in his art.

I also noticed I'd wanted to bring in Tom Wolfe's *The Painted Word* (it was also on the floor), and write about Wolfe's observation: in modern abstract art, what in essence happened is that the art became defined not so much by its own passionate impact, as by the passion of what was said and written about it.

But, hey, maybe not this time. Somehow it didn't seem like it was going to work out that way. I walked toward the kitchen, musing about how to get Jackson Pollock and Tom Wolfe in, when I realized that the Sunday paper was waiting outside.

It's fascinating how much passion there always is in a Sunday *Washington Post*, and this day's was most typical—people damaging each other in every possible manner known to us, Toronto vying with New York as a mecca for theater—and David Koresh post-mortemed to find the seeds of his savage, sad lunacy in the sad life and times of a sad child raised by sad parents.

To make it short, and I *could* go on, I spent a fine morning floating my way around doing this article—not because I dislike writing, not because there was nothing about the concept of passion to write about related to creativity, not because there was no pressure to get it done—but because

I couldn't yet recognize what I wanted to say. In the meantime, I lugged an air conditioner upstairs, ate a piece of cold pizza, waxed a piece of wood on my boat (more, later!), woke my son up, took a shower, and went to church.

It was there that it occurred to me. Passion is what happens when a person is engaged in one thing that embodies what life is about: finding ourselves.

Now, I don't know what Rollo May was writing about in his book, but what occurred to me was that, when you boil it down, anything a person does that gets one's full energy and attention, one's complete, intense emotional commitment, is likely to be something that defines who that person is, and what his or her life is about. People are passionate about things or people or ideas that mean a lot to them; and being passionate, they are usually willing to go through a lot of hell if necessary in order to acquire or safeguard these things. And when you learn what means a lot to a person, or what he or she will do to protect something, or to accomplish something, you know that person a lot better than before. In fact, I think it is *only* when you know what a person will do, that you really know that person.

And this applies to knowing yourself, in spades.

So, in the moment, this is how I found myself: reluctant to write, but wanting to. Reluctant to concentrate, but wanting to. Reluctant, happily—because in my life at the moment on this day were other passions, at least equally powerful in defining to me who I am or want to be. And that, frankly, is how I want it to be for the rest of my life.

The moral of this story? I guess right now, Sunday morning, it is "Go with the flow." As deadlines approach, however, I recognize that the moral changes, at least for me, and becomes "You don't have to like it. You just have to do it." That moral has served me well on many occasions. Here's a final one, for now: "Know yourself better. Do something. *Let* yourself be passionate about it."

Now, about my boat, my present overriding passion.

When our daughter was born, in 1981, I pretty much pulled out of mountain climbing as a pastime, and replaced it with sailing small strange boats. We bought our present one in 1985. It's a little larger than a rowboat, and has three red sails. I found it in a cornfield on the Eastern Shore of Maryland. It was almost ten years old when I bought it.

It is a "cute" boat in that it is little, and good-looking. We named it *Isaiah*. I'd always wanted to name a son Isaiah, but my wife nixed it, except for a boat. I think she figured it would be easier than going through labor again.

Another fact about my boat: a man named Webb Chiles sailed a boat just like it from San Diego to Australia to the Suez Canal to the Canary Islands, before calling it quits. He took about four years to do it.

I worked my butt off this spring, painting, scraping, varnishing, patching—*Isaiah* is a thing of beauty, a floating piece of art now, after years of serviceable dowdiness. As we wander along together this summer people will, as soon as I come into view, know something about me because of my boat—I'm passionate about her, and I sure sail slow. I, of course, already know these things, and they are *very* important facts about me.

Madonna, Chalk on Paper,
24"x18", ©1977, Bruce Holly

Acrylic and Chalk on Paper,
24"x18", ©1985, Bruce Holly

▲ Witness

Art is about being willing to see. And hear. And feel. Art is about not looking away from what the world has to offer, and expressing what happens next. Art is an act of witness.

I watch a lot of TV.

Nightly, I watch vignettes of the day's activities in Saudi Arabia, where people are getting ready to fight, and maybe to die. I watch now with a raptness that I don't remember having as a young man, when I and my compatriots were preparing for potential life and death in Vietnam. Back then, I ignored a lot.

Every hour, and on the half-hour, we can hear and see grand and frightening things, tape-recorded and videotaped for the world to witness at its leisure. As one result, no American with a working radio or television can nowadays fail to identify the beat of a military helicopter or the staccato stammer of machine guns, simply because they serve as everyday background noise to our lives.

We are daily witnesses to violence and other forms of human grief, but at a distance that requires most of us to make a deliberate effort to imagine the full, awesome implications of it. For most of us, the death and maiming of brothers and sisters, fathers and sons in far corners of the world never brings the horrid reality home to us. For most of us, they aren't our brothers and sisters, fathers and sons. For most of us, Vietnam, Saudi Arabia, and other wars in other lands and on our own streets remain, even with today's split-second news coverage, events we know about but don't know.

Most of us feel like we need to protect ourselves from

being overwhelmed by the intensity of certain kinds of events, and we early develop ways of blocking our awareness, or buffering it. We become adept at avoiding "thinking the unthinkable," and being able to stop thoughts that trouble us, and ignoring or distorting aspects of certain experiences which would be likely to throw us for a loop. We develop the ability to turn our gaze away from things that are potentially too intense or uncomfortable for us to bear, much like we avoid staring full at the sun.

Additionally, when we have intense experiences, we often choose to keep them intimate, to be shared with few others. Chuck Pratt, an American rock climber, once wrote that after reaching the top of a difficult climb, he and his partner shared feelings "that were nobody's business but our own." He spoke for many of us in similar situations.

However, there are people among us whose response is different. They look full into the sun, and then convey the experience brilliantly to others. At the risk of being blinded, they see, and through their eyes, we see. When the drums of war roll, they listen to the screams beneath, and through their ears, we hear.

Enter the artist.

From time immemorial, there have been some among us who do not flinch from looking and seeing and experiencing the world around them. Whether the experience is of intense pain, joy, or horror, it is absorbed by these individuals in full measure. The creative work comes in how this experience is then relayed so it becomes available to us all, so that the emotional and spiritual importance is as tangible as the physical evidence of the event. So that we know the event. Through these individuals, we all become witnesses to all of history.

As artists, our individual testimony about life invariably will be unique, if we choose to give it, and will vary from the perceptions of others in almost any and every aspect. But it

Essays on The Psychology of Creativity

is precisely through this sharing of our individual experience that we all can learn of the full meaning of any human event.

In this vein, autobiography is a particularly potent means of converting one's entire life into a creative event, a testimony for others. Some have used autobiography to describe the development of specific contributions in science, politics, or art. Memoirs of great people often serve this purpose. Others have used autobiography to document their interpretation of the meaning of life itself. Some deliberately design their lives as a creative statement about mankind, and use the written word as a means of conveying the statement.

Tristan Jones, a sailor, is one such individual. For years, he has set out on improbable, and in many ways, idiosyncratic quests, from stranding himself in northerly ice floes for years in a small boat, to sailing across South America and Europe. In one sense, his accumulated account of his life in several books is a journal of remarkable sailing adventures. In another sense, it is the creative documentation of one man's living, an extended reportage of his coping with the ordinary feelings, foibles, and distortions that are familiar in each of our own lives. Read in this light, Mr. Jones' books offer us the opportunity to respond strongly to the ordinariness in each of our own lives, our common humanity, despite whatever extraordinary circumstances might be affecting us.

Kathe Kollwitz, a German printmaker during the first half of this century, documented the events of life around her, and used her own self-image to convey emotions that were also explosively expressed during her lifetime in the Russian Revolution and other proletarian-led efforts to change the existing old order in Europe. In stark, ruthless simplicity, Kollwitz rendered images of human pain, grief, and suffering that hurt even now to behold—of workers, children, and women whose cries become concrete in her charcoals, lithographs, and etchings.

But it is in her self-portraits that Kollwitz gives us the means to appreciate the effect of the times on a real person, and allows us to viscerally sense the depth of the pain of a horrendous era in Western European history.

Kollwitz drew few portraits, *per se*, and most were of herself. In them, the image of a plain, simply dressed woman, an almost generic mother figure drawn in broad, strong lines, and dark, brooding, subtle charcoal chiaroscuro, reappears through time in poses of bone-deep weariness, resignation, and grief. And yet, in each self-portrait, her eyes are open—steadily, resignedly, unflinchingly open to the world that confronts her at the moment.

In Kollwitz's work, we the audience have two potential viewpoints: we see what she sees, or we see her seeing it. And through our view of her as witness, we witness.

In every era of human history, people with creative courage have made powerful works of witness in similar fashion. In our own time, the act of witness as a creative response to often unbearable events is nowhere so clear as in the art, literature, and philosophy which grew out of the Holocaust. From the hidden pictures of the doomed artists of Terezin to the later works of survivors such as Elie Wiesel and Viktor Frankl, we as a people can learn what we must learn about ourselves—we are capable of doing things far more intensely good or evil than we are willing, without assistance, to witness.

Art holds us accountable, across time.

▲ Sublimation

Traditional psychoanalysis views art as a process of displacing the expression of primitive, direct, instinctual drives into forms which are more socially acceptable. This process is referred to as sublimation. Arguably a limited notion of the creative process, it is nonetheless useful to contemplate.

Sublimation is distinct from simple displacement of effort or attention. Sublimation implies a significant alteration or expansion of focus and goals, and an intense encounter with some aspect of the artist's life. Displacement, on the other hand, has a more defensive function in that it helps one avoid facing particular problems or issues.

In the half-light of human awareness, artists become facilitators. Images are brought from the threshold of consciousness—the field of not-yet-known possibilities—into perceptible forms. At times, these forms become sublime in their power to inspire deep feeling, even awe or exaltation.

Edith Kramer, an artist, author, and therapist, describes sublimation in art as a "largely unconscious transformation of feeling into form." In Kramer's view, artists are faced with two general problems in their work. First is the search for subject matter which is engaging. Then there is the struggle to give it a form which expresses the tensions of the engagement—encompassing the private experience or feeling of the encounter—in a format accessible to others.

The artistic process is by nature pleasurable. Psychologist and philosopher Rollo May speaks of this intrinsic pleasure as joy in one's potential becoming actualized. But it is not always satisfying. Kramer points out that the pleasure of creative sublimation is often more lasting and "exquisite" than the pleasure in direct gratification of hunger, sexuality, aggression, and the like. Yet, she says, artistic pleasure cannot be as intense, because one must renounce *complete* gratification of instincts in order to have energy available to create.

In Kramer's words, "Artist and audience travel together in two directions, from the primitive source of the creative impulse toward its final form, and again from the contemplation of form to the depth of complex, contradictory, and primitive emotions."

This assertion has an existential connotation that is at the core of what art provides us as humans. To paraphrase poet Stanley Kunitz's words, the hard inescapable phenomena to be faced is that we are living and dying at once. Our commitment is to report that dialogue. Simply put, we share this reality: we are all born to die.

This fact of life consciously or unconsciously organizes our every action and thought, throughout our lives. We have a basic instinct to *live*, over and above mere survival. Ultimately, it is this instinct which provides us with the core of our creative power, and—in a sense—with our central mission as artists.

In our will to live, we have the energy available to cope with mortality in the present, and the force to bridge to past and future generations. Art provides us with a means to convert our instinctive responses—our wishes, desires, and will to live—into products which live forever, beyond our own mortal ends.

In art, we transcend time.

Imagine a tree. Imagine looking through a lens, up through branches. Imagine these branches growing, splitting, splaying, in fast-motion.

A child is born. The child branches out, lean and supple. Have the sounds and soft words, the warm, wet piquancy of infancy left their marks on memory and personality? The harsh experiences? You bet.

Scroll forward a bit—the tears of adolescence frame eyes that behold a world with parts unsafe, parts unfair. He has all the accoutrements of growth—friends, enemies; stubbed fingers, accomplished hands; failing parents, growing siblings.

Through the rolling moaning fast motion, images stick, some pinned firm to his memory, some hanging at the edge of consciousness, tenuous as eggs on a shaky table. Some—they have a half-glimpsed sheen that distracts the eye—are almost hidden by the darkness in the cracks of the mind into which they have fallen.

Are the images recorded? Yes. Replayed? Mercy, yes. He paints, drawing out tube-thick lines to mark the edges of the images.

But which way is the flow? His life, recorded beneath awareness, every branching way—is that the source?

He grows older. The body of work is mature, too. Many artworks; universal messages, in unique vessels. His work has had its changing tempos: long, airy pauses; misshaped passages; missed notes; tortured, awkward beats. And phrases of clarion beauty, clear as crystal, its moments hearkening to immortality.

Long after he dies, his paintings—his experiences made immortal—are like branches, intertwining with the searching limbs of other children of the world. They are seen by other sons and daughters, and they intertwine with their lives, their own private half-shaped visions.

Which way does life flow now? Core to branch and back to core—the gaps fill in. The universe expands.

▲ THE OBSERVING SELF

Artists are active observers. We become aware of our experience of life, and in some fashion we act on the awareness. Sometimes this means we pay attention to our interior feelings and paint, or dance, or act, in consonance with them. Sometimes we become willing to confront, experience, and express our perceptions and interpretations of the universe around us. And sometimes we allow ourselves to see, feel, or touch parts of ourselves and our world that we and our fellows consciously would rather avoid.

There is a raw, basic quality to life that exists with elemental intensity and power in each of us. Most of us spend much of our lives attempting to shape and buff this rawness into socially acceptable, personally comfortable dimensions. We must do this as a matter of course in order to make life tolerable. Otherwise, we would be constantly grappling with the razor-edge issues of reality, at every moment aware of the animal violence and pain surrounding us as we stand in apparently serene forest glades, unable to bathe happily in our occasional fountains of joy because of the next dry sad season we so assuredly expect.

Of the many ways we employ to cope with this intensity, I think one of the most interesting is our ability to stand outside ourselves in our experience of life. Our ability as human beings to do so protects us from being overwhelmed by feelings, painful events, and catastrophe, and it allows us to clarify the meaning of those events for ourselves. Moreover, the ability to do art is, I believe, a functional expression of this ability to experience, observe, and act as if from a detached perspective.

We have a varied vocabulary to describe this

phenomenon. When a doctor is able to sew up a child's gash in spite of the child's cries, whimpers, and obvious pain, we speak of his "professional detachment." We are struck numb by grief when a loved one dies, yet are able to graciously handle the chores and social demands of a wake and funeral, though at times feeling "as if in a dream." We read of the "out-of-body" experiences of the dying. We talk of "getting a grip" on ourselves, "stepping back" from a situation to view it more clearly, or being "beside ourselves" from the intensity of an emotion.

As in most things human, there is the potential for pathology in our ability to dissociate aspects of ourselves from the events at hand. To live constantly "as if in a dream" is unsettling, and past a certain point it brings many people into therapy. To feel like the events of one's daily life are not quite real is to experience a loss, which when continuous is seriously disorienting. These conditions are referred to psychiatrically as depersonalization disorders when they are persistent and severe enough to cause discomfort and concern. Other related psychiatric conditions include psychogenic fugue, the abrupt leaving of one's home or work, forgetting one's past, and assumption of a new identity. Psychogenic amnesia, the loss of a portion of one's personal history, also occurs with some frequency. And most of us are familiar, from accounts such as *The Three Faces of Eve*, with multiple personality disorder, wherein a person develops several distinct and separate personalities, each with his or her own perceptions, behavior patterns, and attitudes.

For most of us, however, self-observation in the form of "stepping outside ourselves" is a consciously used tool in business, athletic performance, and in relationships. In psychotherapy, and especially in hypnosis, there are many times when a patient is asked to become aware of himself from a new perspective, or to lend aid to himself as if he were dealing with a separate person. Art and literature are replete with the work of people in extremis, using their talents in the service of gaining some personal detachment and giving meaning to their experiences. When a dying man makes a journal entry he becomes a chronicler of life, rather than simply a victim.

Sometimes, in often very interesting or significant ways, our ability to project our awareness and point of view outside ourselves manifests itself in *déjà vu* types of experiences. We observe ourselves having an eerily familiar experience, and at times we cannot clearly perceive the chain of associations or memories that link immediate events to our past experience. In some cases, there is no discernible link. In others, the link immediately becomes obvious. One characteristic of these experiences seems to be that our sense of "observer status" in the immediate situation is heightened.

I can offer a personal example of this sensation of observer status.

I used to be a paratrooper. The Army unit I was with tended to jump in small units, often at night. One day, however, I climbed onto a plane with soldiers from another branch of the service. The plane approached our drop zone, and I jumped out, along with the others in our group. After a few seconds, my parachute opened with a jerk, and I looked around. Suddenly, the experience was transformed for me. It was as if I had a front row seat in a movie, rather than actually being suspended in a chute harness several hundred feet in the air. The bright sky was filled with hundreds of parachutists, from many airplanes. Almost immediately, I was aware that the scene around me was associated with photographs I'd seen as a child of mass parachute drops during World War II. I was filled with childlike awe and I felt like a spectator. At the same time, I was aware of my own sensations and feelings, and noticed that it took some effort on my part to accept the reality of my own participation in the drop.

Artists share this most human ability to observe a scene and to include themselves in the observation. Artists take the experience one step further: they act on it, and make it concrete and communicable to others.

Some artists are consciously self-observant, and their art is an expression of their self-perception of emotions, sensations, and thoughts. Self-portraiture is a good example of this form of self-observation, and common is the artist's using himself as a model on occasion.

Others literally include themselves in the scenes they depict, often as spectators: Michelangelo's self-image appears in the frescoes of the Sistine Chapel ceiling, present at the Creation. The French Impressionists painted themselves and each other into street scenes, often painting each other painting the Paris scene, and so on.

There is also another form of self-observation, the unconscious activity we call intuition. For some artists, the activity of art is in itself the art. The apparent spontaneity and immediate energy of some abstract art arises from the artist intuitively, without conscious thought, or in some cases, in spite of it. In other cases, an artist makes an aesthetically pleasing piece without being able to consciously account for the piece's success. The artist is unaware of being anything other than a vehicle for the expression. Yet, in all of these cases, the basic, key factor is that the artist puts himself at the service of creative activity, in essence observing himself as "Artist" at the critical juncture in history when the artwork in question could appear.

Art, then, can be seen as the tangible expression of human beings willing to observe in themselves the creative potential that exists in all humanity. We can use our ability to stand outside ourselves consciously as a tool for new perspectives, and we can use our ability to observe our interior motives as a means to put ourselves in the path, at the right time, of creativity waiting to happen. In either case we have an ability which distinguishes us from all other living beings.

▲ ART, AMBIGUITY, AND AMBIVALENCE: GENIUS AS THE ABILITY TO LIVE WITH WAFFLING

At my daughter's school, they treat the study of Latin like it is a contact sport. They play for blood, in team competitions complete with cheerleaders, Latin stars, franchise players—at the school, state, and national levels. My daughter knows seventh graders whose grasp of the history, mythology, syntax and arcane rhythms of Latin beats my grasp of English. Folks familiar with my writing may at this point remark that my grasp of English is not particularly firm, but please, take my point here.

These kids are whizzes at a language whose speakers hammered much of Western civilization into shape two thousand years ago before collapsing beneath their own weight, with the help of a Visigoth invasion or two. Today these children casually chat away in a tongue most familiar to folks who became dust thousands of years ago.

Many of my daughter's classmates are gifted classics scholars by the time they get their driver's licenses, and they look, act, and in day-to-day conversation, sound like your average Bill and Jessica, Ming-Wei, Luigi, Andrew, and Yaksha. They can and often do play football or Nintendo with the same fierce seriousness and skill and youthful abandon, and forget their lunches, and play music with 'way too much bass emphasis, and order frightening varieties of pizza. They move among their peers with the easy insouciance of top jocks everywhere, veterans of fierce dog-eat-dog competitions where pressure, psychological intimidation, and high drama weigh heavily in the air as they struggle to answer questions about obscure, long-forgotten Roman skirmishes in Judea, or to recall the first three words in a poem by Catullus. Their answers often have the all-or-nothing importance of last-second tie-breaking field goals. Winning isn't easy, and these kids are winners.

Have you ever watched a group of such kids try to answer a really tough question in heavy head-to-head Latin competition? I tell you, it's the stuff of legend.

Unlike a lot of adults, most kids don't waste a lot of energy trying to hide what they go through, so it is right there for anyone to watch. They look up in pleading to the heavens; they shift their eyes back and forth as if in search of rescue. They start to speak, then hesitate. They murmur, they sigh, they wring their hands, they fidget ... and then, in the last instant before the buzzer, as if resigning themselves to hopeless, futile stabs in the dark—often even when they are pretty sure of themselves—they offer their answers as if they were questions ("—Is ... Is the answer 'Marcus Aurelius'?").

Their anxious discomfort is often palpable—and painful to behold—until they receive some sign from the almighty Judge that—("Score!")—they got it right! That their answer is, among all the possibilities they'd run through their minds—the one *right* answer! Then relief, exhilaration, satisfaction wash over them like a warm blast of air—until the next question. And on and on, with one tough question after another, each with its own right answer—until one team emerges from the fray, flushed with victory like casually dressed and underage gladiators.

It is an exquisite process to behold.

The process also serves well to illustrate, in a nutshell, the core of the creative process: toleration of ambivalence and ambiguity followed by a decision to act.

But there is one difference between the competition of these young Latin lions and the general process of creativity—and it makes all the difference in the world.

By and large, in the world of Latin scholarship, there are right answers, and wrong answers, and in most instances, *only* one correct answer, to a specific question. In the wider arena of human experience, this is most often not so. Most human questions have many possible answers, all equally valid.

Absolutes are very, very rare in rational human life. It seems we humans have to rely on faith and revelation to provide us with absolute bedrock. And most of us need bedrock to ground ourselves and to contain the chaos surrounding us so we can tolerate being alive without going mad.

However, without spiritual resources, we are forced to contend naked with a universe filled with alternate possibilities and often conflicting alternatives. When physicists finally discover the so-called "Theory of Everything," for instance, which explains the behavior of the universe from the subatomic level to the cosmic level, it is likely that they will have to deal with the notion that there may well be two or more such Theories, and that they can't be sure which one is operating at any given time.

So too with human relationships. It is the rare lover who at some moment does not both adore and despise his or her beloved, or realize that he or she is only one of many possible loves. Moreover, it is the rare saint who is not an accomplished sinner, and the rare sinner who has absolutely no claim worthy of canonization. So too with all life.

In practice, living seems to be about making choices and then tolerating the notion that things *could* at any point be different. It is also about dealing with a subtle and ever-present realization we each have that every decision we make is not only not black-and-white but may be Technicolor as well as a shade of gray.

Art is the expression of this struggle by individuals among us willing to take the struggle one step beyond awareness, and to make it concrete. Ambiguity, the possibility of alternative significances, is as integral an aspect of all art as ambivalence, the experience of often conflicting possibilities and feelings, is a part of all life. And the core dilemma of human development, of all learning, and of all creative criticism is: how do we nurture our tolerance for ambiguity and ambivalence as the first step in nurturing ourselves and each other as truly creative individuals?

The ability to perceive ambiguity in art and in life comes with experience. The ability to tolerate ambivalence comes with maturity. And creativity arises from the ability to cherish both.

▲ At the Moment

Let me tell you about my favorite dream. In it, I am flying along, about a foot off the ground, as if I were suspended beneath an invisible car. I'm gliding cross-country at a steady, comfortable speed over roads that twist and turn through the kind of country I associate with Ireland, with hedges and hillocks and vistas of rolling grass and sky. Whatever the surface below me, bumpy as it might be, I move silently, sinuously, calmly immersed in a gentle steady journey with no conscious destination ahead. It is a wonderfully soothing dream, and one I call up on purpose occasionally, when I need to relax a bit.

The closest I've come to this experience in real life is on my motorcycle, and then only for brief moments when something seems to click in, and things are, for an instant in time—well, just right. Everything is under control. The road is smooth. I'm in a rhythm that fits. And in that moment, I feel completely safe and at peace for a little bit of eternity.

In one such moment recently, I got a sense of what it might be like to be a bit of sentient paint at the end of a moving brush, gliding through the landscape of a painting in the making. I was out for a joyride along a dirt road under the late evening sun of a Virginia summer day. The smell of honeysuckle was like an invisible wall in the warm air. Green abounded in every field and stand of oak, maple, and cedar I passed, shades and tones of green beyond counting, greens beyond belief. (I say: to learn about the color green, come to Virginia in mid-summer.) And in the shimmering evening light, shadows fell in front of me like hazy lace in the dust of the road. The scene around me was filled with an abundance of texture, from the rippled fields coarse with half-grown corn to the soft, gauzy air through which I rushed, to the emotional textures within my own mind as the road and I flowed together from curve to curve.

It dawned on me that the landscape, from where I saw it, was like the impastoed surface of a canvas which had been painted and repainted many, many times. Each flash of color, each skimming retinal image touched an emotional chord in me—I say this on faith, because in the moment, I was only aware of fleeting half-thoughts, half-hungers, half-longings flashing by just beyond the speed at which I might recognize them. Each sensation seemed related both to a personal history I brought into the scene within myself at sixty miles an hour on an aging motorbike—and to the fertile, constantly renewing, eons-old history of the land around me at the moment.

It was as if I were immersed in a music from so deep within myself I could only know it was there, without hearing it consciously. And for an instant, I became part of the texture, part of the color around me, and my music became part of the music of the land, part of that moment which lives now for me in memory as one of the subtly intense "nows" that are like islands—or more accurately, like beacons for me when I find myself at sea in life searching for the moments at which things seem—well, just right.

This might seem a tad mystical-magical, a bit too much, you might say. But tell me you haven't had similar experiences.

For some, being clicked into such a moment comes at times of high passion or danger. For others it comes upon facing a canvas, or a piece of stone, or a typewriter. For some, it comes out of a pipe or a bag of mushrooms—for a price.

For most of us, such moments come unpredictably, but they seem to come most often when we commit ourselves to something that seems important to us. It is not clear why this is so, but it seems more true to me than most other "facts" of life I've learned over time.

With care and love, even one such moment's worth of joy or beauty can be enough to make life worth living. The warmth in our world that nurtures such moments comes from within ourselves, and is shared between us when we share being alive, *now*, with each other. The open human heart warms its own kind more truly than any sun, here.

In contrast, a stingy, cruel emotional climate can make even the most breathtaking morning sun seem only like the rising of hell itself. Some say a closed heart is a fortress; some say it is a prison. Some say it is an empty hole. Few hearts are deliberately locked by their owners, but many are frozen shut by a cold fear of being rejected, by the chill of past disappointments and hurts, and by the quiet winter of unspoken, unheard longing.

Thankfully, among us, throughout time, pass individuals possessed with the grace and courage to lead by example in their abandonment of reserve, their ability to live in the moment, their willingness to know and be known, and their ability to convey what they learn of life. Some are known as saints, some are seen as sinners. All in their own way are artists. Some become exalted for their example, while others are martyred for it. Either way, the effect of their lives keeps us alive as a race, and by their examples we each are empowered to extend human history with our own unique offerings of experiences.

The other day a friend of mine called my attention to the fact that on average, in our land, human beings live about 25,000 days or so. That seemed a small number to him in that context, and I agreed. Then I figured out that I have, actuarially speaking, about 10,000 days left myself. The clock really started ticking louder then.

Whether we have 10,000 mornings left, or ten, or one, we have an eternity ahead of us if we are engaged in the sharing of heart that lives on. Art, even at its most painful and brutal, is a sharing of the love between ourselves and

Bruce M. Holly

life itself. By being around for even one more sun, we each have another chance to create the world anew. And as artists, we have a high road available between the rich land within ourselves and the world around us. It is a road with twists and blind alleys, for sure, but it is a path worth following, every step of the way.

▲ Transitions

Here is a truth—human existence is an exercise in going from here to there in some fashion. Psychology is the study of how we cope with the experience. Our sciences, our art, literature, drama, dance—are how we record our efforts and attempt to fathom their meaning.

You might even say, making transitions between things is what life is really about, and the nodal events and experiences that seem so important in themselves are like ledges on a rock climb, insignificant except as resting points on the way, or catalysts for further progress, or boundary zones marking either the beginning or end of difficulties.

More truth. There is no flat way to high places. Along the rugged highways of life, a relatively few weary pilgrims search for glimmers of wisdom, for the soft glow of meaning and logic and direction if nothing else—or more hopefully, for the rock-solid brilliance of revealed, immutable truth, available only to those whose faith in the limits of chaos transcend life's available evidence.

We tend to think of these people, who cross boundaries and serve as professional pathfinders for humanity—the scientists, scholars, artists, saints, and seers among us, as our most interesting and bravest souls. They are travellers in the interfaces between light and dark, wrong and right, known and unknown—people at the edge and beyond of what we know and believe.

In contrast, however, many of us live as if "you can't get there from here" is our credo. We stolidly accept the limits that intelligence, economics, and our desire for security place on us. We believe that somehow, the past holds the truest answers for us, and live as if tomorrow is a threat. Staying stock still and cutting our potential losses seems our best bet. The movement of others, while intriguing at times, most often seems somehow dangerous.

Transitions, whether personal or universal in scope, are times of anxiety and unsettled feelings, times when both hope and loss mingle freely in our psyches. The risk of change is the risk of error, the potential for losing what little we've got. The interstices of our human development seem often like the cracks of doom through which we more often glimpse hell than heaven, and most often we have no sense at all of what to expect.

There is a considerable literature about how human beings move through a number of predictable stages on the way to maturity. What is noteworthy is how we tend to move forward ever so tentatively, our movement a flow and ebb wherein we cover the same ground over and over, as if practicing progress before committing ourselves completely.

In my line of work, I have gotten to know a lot of people, mostly women, who are engaged in trying to resolve abusive relationships. Many have been repeatedly abused, physically, emotionally, sexually by partners they genuinely love and believe love them. Very often they are mystified by the patterned dance they seem locked into, a sad ballet of pain, remorse, forgiveness, and renewed tension. Many have repeated the steps of the dance many times, their movements punctuated by events of increasingly severe violence and terror.

Some finally arrive at a point of desperation which allows them to move out of the cycle, in spite of the fear and loneliness and abandonment that inevitably accompany their decisions to act. Some find that by doing so, they enable their partners to come to grips with the reality of the harm they are doing. Eventually they can reunite as couples safely and at a new level of maturity and intimacy. Others find that by facing and weathering their losses, they become free to grow themselves and seek out new relationships that satisfy both their needs and their hopes for mutual caring and respect.

What seems to stand out in my mind about these folks is that their lives become defined not by the events of often horrible pain and cruelty they experience, but by their efforts to change, to transcend the limits imposed on them by circumstances, and to move into new lives where they and their families can be safe and whole. Defined by events, they are victims. Defined by the transitions they make, they are survivors.

In general, as we develop and move through life, we tend to cushion our anxiety with transitional objects at each stage we pass through. These "objects" are similar to the familiar teddy bear or raggedy blanket stand-ins for Momma that comfort a growing toddler. Some of us seek fetishes which serve to alter our perceptions of life and soothe our fears by embodying our images of power and security. Cars and clothes and "correct" friends often serve this purpose. Others of us attempt to anesthetize ourselves against our fear of loss with alcohol or other drugs, or sex, or food. As a species, we are remarkably good at finding a variety of opiates to deaden ourselves against experiences we perceive to be painful.

And for some of us, art serves as a means of both coping with and deepening our experience, even when it is painful. We make creativity itself a means of comfort and of containing as well as expressing the fears and doubts and confusion that accompany movement.

Art is a bridge between experience and understanding. And it is a moving in and of itself, from idea to action and back again. During its creation, an artwork often evolves with a history of changes, of starts and stops and pauses, of fearless, confident, and bold action followed by trepidation and retraction. Each stage is significant as a passage. In a sense, this history forms the soul of the piece. Responding to this,

Picasso once cautioned that the sale of a painting is its death as an evolving thing.

But that seems such a limited view of the life of an artwork. Art evolves not only in response to the action of the artist, but also in response to the vision and intuition of the audience. A piece of music is different at each recital, a play is new each night, and a dance lives as if newborn at each performance precisely for this reason.

This is no less true for literature, and for the visual arts. Witness the painted animals on the walls of the caves of Lascaux. They breathe with life today, thousands of years after their creator has become dust, when we respond to them with understanding and respect. Through an archaic gesture of earthen paint on earthen walls, one human's vision of his world has bridged across centuries to touch our imaginations now. The artist in question ran his course in history eons ago, nasty brutish, and short as it probably was for him. His art possibly served him consciously as a way to transcend his immediate experience, and now, without his knowing or caring, it serves as a direct link between his ancient spirit and our own.

It seems I can't write about this stuff without sounding full of myself—chasing elusive coherence in describing a process I'm in up to my neck in myself seems to do it, I think. I feel like I have to risk acting like I know what I'm talking about to get anywhere at all.

So it goes. The universe is explored by pompous fatheads with ideas they believe in as well as by the humble who stumble on truth, and we're all ever in transition between idiocy and the anointment of genius. Most of the time the best we can do is make guesses about where along the spectrum we happen to be at the moment.

▲ A Leap of Faith

I've been thinking a lot about God lately. I'm in the midst of what has become a chronic crisis of faith. In questioning the beliefs I used to hold so firmly, I'm surprised by a couple of things: I'm not as frightened as I thought I'd be, and I haven't lost my faith that there *is* a God. I just don't know much about Him (or Her, or It ...).

I was raised a Catholic. Today I cling to my Catholicism as a young child on a trip to unfamiliar territory clings to a security blanket. The Church is like a dock I'm not able to cast off from, holding tight to the last line while my boat bobs and weaves in the outgoing tide. I'm sort of on autopilot until things get clearer. There's a philosophical construct I remember hearing about in college—I think it's called "Pascal's Gamble"—that suggests you should act as if there is a God, because if there is, you win, and if there isn't, you haven't lost anything. That sounds a bit like what I'm doing these days. But I remember that as a construct it was heavily criticized, and it does avoid what I see as a basic personal issue in faith: either you believe or you don't. Soren Kierkegaard called it a "leap of faith." I speak and act as if I do believe, but it takes an act of will. And I think I don't. I feel kind of like a cartoon character who finds himself in mid-leap over a canyon and scrambles back in mid-air to the edge of the cliff. I'm back on the brink, staring at the jump again.

I'm also in the middle of preparing to give a speech to a large group of artists about the creative intersection of art, artists, and audiences. And I'm running into the same dilemma as I do with God. I'm balking at the leap of faith it takes to feel that the ideas I'm still forming have any real relevance to art, artists, and audiences.

Part of it is stage fright. I'm sure that when I scrabble to the podium in a couple of weeks, I will be a totally terrified individual, about to be greeted warmly by people who in short order will want to gnaw my bones, or—worse—will stare impassively at me while I self-destruct before their eyes. At least, that's the mental scene I have to wade through each time I start to work on the speech, before I breathe deeply, shake myself, and imagine myself talking to a hall full of naked people. But then that doesn't help either. I either end up in a giggling fit or get turned on, neither of which helps me concentrate.

In the past, speaking in public seemed easier for me. But that may have been because I was living in a bubble of self-confidence blown around me by my own ignorance. I'd underorganize my speeches and lectures, precisely because my ideas were underorganized—and I would hope that my audiences would self-select what they needed or wanted to hear. Kind of like putting on a verbal smorgasbord. Maybe something would stick out as making sense; or someone, in responding to what I threw out, would help me sort it out for myself. But often, I'd leave a number of confused, dissatisfied people in my wake, including myself.

Now, as a means of developing and refining ideas, batting around a few half-baked notions in a group is not a bad way to go about things. But one really ought to do it with people who are informed—consenting participants in a brainstorming session. Most people showing up for a Saturday morning lecture at a conference tend to expect, and deserve, something a bit more sifted out by the speaker.

What I'm realizing is that when it comes to what I'm most often asked to discuss, the creative process, my own ideas often contradict themselves and change over time. For instance, I've vilified critics when they concentrate on judging artwork rather than focusing on art as a personal and social process. Then I've turned around and excoriated the schlock art that exudes from some people like phlegm.

So in the end, the best I can do is define what I'm thinking at the moment as clearly as I can, hope it's of some interest to someone, and further, hope that my thinking will be accepted as a work in progress.

I started off working on this speech by going through a bunch of old articles, looking for classy phrases and ideas which I could cut and paste together to say something about how artists use their inner lives as a means of understanding the world around them, and how the art they produce is a documentation of the process. I wanted to say something about the various intersections of experience that provide us with most of our creative opportunities: our inner and outer worlds, our conscious and unconscious lives, the present moment as an intersection of past and future, the unique individual as someone with something universal to say—that sort of thing. I wanted to talk about the personal borders most artists have to cross in order to become and remain creatively productive—boundaries of fear of exposure, technical limitations, the discomfort of witnessing uncomfortable aspects of life, awe at the potency of life itself. I wanted to say something useful about the role of criticism in helping both artist and audience become more productive.

Above all, I wanted to grab and fascinate the people I'd be talking to; I wanted them to love me; I wanted them to run out of the lecture hall and go searching for art materials like addicts scrambling for their fixes.

Not bad for forty-five minutes followed by questions.

Now, three-and-a-half drafts later, I have a vast bucket of a speech, which gives me some hope of success in saying a few cogent things, if I can boil it down from raw sap into something pungent and rich. In between bouts with the word processor, I entertain myself with visions of us all having an uproariously good time as I fly around the stage yakking like

Mr. Wizard on speed. I find myself rewriting a little less each time I plow through what I'm going to say, and growing a bit more self-confident with each rehearsal. I'm still having occasional panic attacks, triggered by flashbacks to previous forays when I spoke like I was on acid and Nembutal and the audience responded, in Arsenio Hall's words, like the cast of "Coma." But the panic attacks are growing less intense.

A leap of faith still lies before me, however, and will come at the instant I walk onto the stage. Will I *believe* in what I have to say, or will I merely think it sounds pretty good?

This is what I believe today: God is a patron of the arts. He will protect the artists I must address. Their time is too precious to Him to let me waste it.

That helps.

▲ That Thin Raw Edge

When I was about nine, my father took me with him on a drive from Maryland to California, where he had been born and lived as a child. We were on the road for about two weeks then; thirty-five years later, I can still remember almost every place we stayed and meal we ate on that trip. It was a crystallizing adventure for me, an experience that shaped my life and my relationship with my old man as surely as a wind shapes the form of a flower or the lay of the land.

This summer, I found myself with several weeks on my own. My wife, son, and daughter all had plans which took them in different directions, and for the first time in three decades, I had a substantial chunk of time to do with as I alone pleased.

I asked my father if he cared to take a drive with me again. He did, and so we hit the road together.

I am in my mid-forties. I have been working essentially full-tilt at being a social worker, therapist, husband, and father for the past twenty years or so. In all these endeavors, the most important tool I have is my ability to understand and appreciate the experience of another human being—empathy, it is called. And like most tools, it requires care, and occasional repair.

By early this summer, I was getting pretty pooped. I felt ready and needful of a break. I also felt kind of glazed over, callused up, and a bit distant from people in general.

Part of me figured it was because finally I was an experienced professional, able to distinguish between myself and others, and competent at knowing whose problem was whose. I also figured it came as a natural, and probably necessary, result of having heard a lot of painful things, and scary things, and sad, mournful things that happened to people, and of having found myself often less useful than either they or I wished I could be.

But, there was another part of me that recognized I was getting less responsive to people in pain and anxiety and that while as a result I might have the ability to see choices invisible to the person fully in the soup of an intense experience, it might also keep me from knowing, in many cases, the full extent of the problem at hand.

In short, I was feeling dull and tired. Not good. Trust me, you don't want a dull brain surgeon, plumber, or psychotherapist working with you. Each can wreak his or her own special kind of havoc. Whatever professional help you need, make sure it is awake and aware.

Traveling is how I personally wake up.

It starts for me in packing. I try to pare things down to essentials, and once on the roll, I move things around again and again until I have what I really need together in a small pack. I usually get a pang of bittersweet satisfaction at how small a bundle it is.

Once that's done, I become free to think thoughts as I drive—I usually drive on trips—that pare things down to emotional essentials for me. It usually isn't long before I am aware of feelings growing in an intensity that I associate almost exclusively with being on the road—feelings of longing, of loneliness, of desire, of hopefulness, of fear, and in the end, of almost overwhelming joy—at times, of rapture.

I'm not exaggerating. I'm not kidding.

It is a most powerful and precious and predictable process for me.

This is why I wanted to travel again with my father. The longing, loneliness, desire, and hopefulness I felt toward him as a young child have changed across time, and yet I needed to know him, and know where I stood with him, now as much as ever before. And as a hone to remove calluses and complacency from my ability to feel and see and understand, I couldn't think of a more useful experience than living day to day and hour to hour with one of my parents for a spell.

And I was right.

The people I work with rightly expect me to be able to meet and accept them at the raw edge of their lives, because it is at that thin raw edge that they must begin to heal. I am paid and I choose to live as a person willing and able to provide my part of this healing interface. It's a tough balance, because on the one hand, I can't be so raw myself that any touch sparks my own overriding pain—yet my skin can't be so thick that I feel none of the pain myself that so often accompanies real intimacy with another person.

The skin under a callus is alive with nerve endings. The creative use of the pain and pleasure they can report is what gives us the potential for changing the things that rub us rather than simply growing inured to them.

We'd been on the road for two days. Through the windshield, the flowers seemed like cones of yellow yearning toward the morning light, wavering and surging in the steady wind. I noticed the first of them in east Texas, growing in ragged long-lined clumps in the parched roadside ditches as we passed towards Austin at seventy miles an hour. I felt mesmerized by the bright spots of yellow on their erratic stalks, and sketched them into my journal in snatches, trying to match my gaze to their passing for a millisecond of focus over and over again as we rushed by.

I thought to ask my father to stop so I could snap off a bloom and stalk and have it to examine at my leisure, but decided against it. It seemed like cheating. And moreover, it would have interrupted the flow of things, and the warm silence that enveloped us for hours at a time.

Black-eyed Susans in a hot west wind on a Texas

Bruce M. Holly

morning, caught in a fleeting glance—so good to see, if you get your eyes just right.

▲ Convergence

One day when my son was a little boy, he began teaching me about the pursuit of illusion. I was preparing to leave on a mountain climbing trip. He brought me a jar, and asked me to bring back some of the clouds he'd heard I would be going through.

I failed my son on that trip. I'm not sure I took his request seriously. I know I brought no clouds home in a jar. A few years later, though, I took him up a mountain with me, and he encountered the clouds for himself. He never told me whether he had been able to fill his own jar, but he did take one with him.

On another more recent day, a drippy, cold one, I was sitting with him on a wet ski lift when illusion and reality converged for me. We had been skiing in a rainstorm, an activity that viewed from one step back is as absurd as any human activity can hope to be. Human technology has made it possible for thousands upon thousands of ill-prepared and generally unaware people to ascend steep mountains in mid-winter, soaking wet, while pretending that they are as safe in doing so as if they were in a bowling alley.

In an attempt to squeeze one more slushy run out of a gloomy day that was getting colder by the minute, we hopped on a lift that was slipping and lurching due to the ice forming on its cables.

The lift hesitated several times on the way up, until toward the top of the mountain, swaying high above scrubby trees coated with a gleaming sheath of rime, we skidded to a solid halt.

In the cloudy darkness, rising wind, and pouring rain, we sat suspended, too high up to jump to the snow, and fully exposed to the wild reality of a northern mountain. We were both wet to the skin, and the rain was beginning to freeze as it landed on us. I looked at my son sitting quietly next to me and realized that if the lift failed to move soon, we were in big trouble. Hypothermia waits for no man or boy, and we were prime candidates for it, along with hundreds of other people spread with abandon across the mountain face. I've cut frozen people out of trees at the base of mountain gullies. I know humans freeze as solid as freezer beef, given time.

The lift finally shuddered into motion, and in due time we slid, cold but safe, back home. But for a brief time, the illusion of safety had become one with the reality of the winter storm, a thin hypnotic veil across the cold rock and ice that formed the mountain on which we were playing.

Epiphanies are funny things. They can be intellectual, yielding glowing insights and understandings. They can be visceral, wordless experiences that illuminate the world and make us part of an intangible unity. They are usually memorable, often highly personal, and can be subtle as well as intense.

Consider how we seek epiphany. Some among us, like Jack London, go out looking for it with a club, rather than awaiting its arrival. Others of us wait with hope and faith. Some are struck down by it, like Paul on the way to Damascus, as we move unsuspecting through life. Some count on sudden leaps to perfection, while others of us are content to crawl slowly towards it. Some of us can live with approximations, others can settle for nothing less than the ultimate.

Art makes epiphany communicable. Through art, artists can make the vision of God available to us all, rather than merely providing a graphic description of their own personal ecstasy. Art is evidence of the convergence of a variety of experiences, part of a process that allows both artist and audience to transcend both illusion and reality, and gain understanding of the truth that flows unseen between the banks of either.

Artists are a culture's lightning rods for revelation, and sensors of the currents and ground swells that are born in the confluence of ideas and experiences and causes and effects that give rise to creativity. They are also human society's lenses by which the moment at hand can be seen as clearly and completely as possible. And as lenses, they are like magnifying glasses in the hands of children on a hot sunny day—they can focus attention and spark, with the intensity of a burning sun, the creative or destructive fire of millions of people's own passionate energies and desires.

Time itself is a part of this convergence as well. And art is a means of transcending time in the communication of felt experience between human beings.

In several of Kurt Vonnegut's novels, a character named Kilgore Trout appears. Among other things, Mr. Trout has an exquisite understanding of time, and timelessness. One of his notions, at least in my mind, is that at any given moment, we exist simultaneously as the infants, children, adolescents, adults, and aged people we were and will be, and that our present manifestation in the Now is no less and no more real than any of our other self-stages. What we now appear like, and perceive others as, is merely the convergence of who we were with who we will be.

I love this image. I use it in my psychotherapeutic work with people. It sometimes gets very interesting when I try to keep it in mind while working with families. It helps make sense of a heck of a lot of otherwise very confusing and often painful behavior.

Similarly, art itself at its best is a tangible communication of what is happening at the confluence of known and unknown, real and illusion, past and future. Art itself is part of a continuum, and the art yet to be created in the far reaches of the future, by artists whose gene pools are as yet far from being filled, is as real in this moment as the fertility fetishes created by our earliest fathers and mothers.

It's easy to understand how, if this is so, even the most humble of artists, with the most modest of personal goals, might have a gut sense of the importance of his chosen activity. While the creation of art is one of the most personal and intimate of human activities, it is also one of the most meaningful and powerful of human endeavors on a societal level. No aware person is likely, given this, to free themselves completely of a sense of awe in embarking in such work.

In the same sense, this may also shed light on why so many artists seem able to diverge from the norm, to be free spirits, free thinkers, and in general, proponents of freedom in its most general sense, relative to their brothers and sisters in any given generation. Anyone who is willing to summon the moral courage necessary to work on a personal expression that transcends history itself simply in the doing of it is likely to be able to speak out on other issues of historically more limited, localized import. Comparatively, these other things do kinda seem like small potatoes.

I love my son. The boy I am likes him as a friend. The father I am is proud of him. The artist I am is filled with hope and desire for him as a work in progress. The old man I am misses him already.

▲ Revisiting the Familiar

P lowing ground twice often makes for richer crops. No matter what the dimensions of our known territory, either in the world around us or within ourselves, passing the same way more than once is often valuable. Monet looked at the same haystacks many times; Van Gogh looked often into his own eyes; Degas advised, "Do the same drawing over and over again and again."

The art of the printer especially lends itself to revisiting. "Vision and Revision," an exhibition of hand-colored prints by Wayne Thiebaud, recently came to Washington. Using 40 years' worth of print proofs, Thiebaud reworked and revised initially similar images over and over in a study of the distinction between a "complete" picture and a "finished" one. Thiebaud writes:

> This ability to understand and determine completeness is part of the human capacity for empathy: by that I mean our ability to transfer ourselves into things—such as paintings and prints—and to actually feel their physical properties. This is a particularly important kind of empathic vitality requiring an openness to experience .... In contrast, finishing off demands a neat typing together of things in a way we "think" is correct. This tends to deaden a work .... Absolute resolution can be dangerously close to the art of taxidermy.

I think what Thiebaud was describing applies to the way people tend to focus their time and energy in living life.

Until recently, and it may still be true, the vast majority

of people on Earth died having no personal experience of the world that was any further than fifty miles from their birthplaces. Most of us have definite and usually quite limited geographical areas in which we visit and revisit scenes and situations over and over. The twists and turns of the land become intimately familiar and we are conscious immediately of any change that happens.

Within the boundaries of our part of the world, we pass again and again along familiar routes, past familiar landmarks. This is true not only of the physical part of this home territory, but also the emotional and spiritual aspects. We tend to stay within the familiar by instinctive choice, and changes usually happen slowly. Most of us by nature seek the comforting security of being settled, of having no reason to go any further, of being done looking for answers. And we use talismans to help us remember what we've got, and what our limits are.

A pocket road atlas is such a talisman for me. With one, I have what I need to bring back a million memories. But I really only need three or four of the pages in my atlas. If you turn to the two-page spread that shows the continental U.S. and begin to work your way west from the Atlantic toward California, you won't go an inch before you've crossed the strip of Earth where I've lived most of my life. When you think about it, that makes me pretty typical. I've personally seen only a tiny piece of this tiny little world as we circle a relatively tiny little sun in the midst of a comparatively small galaxy in an out-of-the-way cove of the universe. My brothers, the Mongol peasant and Pygmy bushman, and I have much in common in our mutual ignorance of what's over the horizon.

I know a fellow who travels on business about two weeks a month. He goes to just about every continent on Earth, it seems, at least once a year. My guess is he uses a globe the way I use a map of the East Coast.

On the other hand, I've known people who would likely

Essays on The Psychology of Creativity

be hopelessly lost once they left the city limits of their hometown. However, within those limits, given a first name and a rough estimate of age of anyone who had lived there in recent memory, they could navigate to the homes of every relative that person had, for three generations back.

When I was a young soldier in training I heard about one American prisoner of war in Korea who kept himself absorbed through month upon month of solitary confinement by drawing a map of his beloved New Jersey in the dirt floor of his jail cell. In that rough map, he could locate the memory of enough warmth and caring and beauty to sustain him through the cruelest of captive winters.

Each of us has a scale of life, it seems, and once we figure out what it is and accept it, it is like a gift and a curse. We become able to focus on what we have in front of us or within easy reach, but in the balance, we tend to lose the restless need that makes it possible to push far beyond familiar horizons. We become able to focus on the abundant history and experience that visits every square foot of soil we individually inhabit, but the time we spend doing it comes out of the limited allowance of hours we have to live, time which others spend in getting from here to "there" at the edge of human experience.

There is yet another focus—the world within each of us. And here, the same is true. Some of swim most comfortably at the surface of ourselves. Some of us will spend everything it takes to dive as deeply as possible into who we are at the core of our beings.

For each of us, living creatively means using what we've got. Some of us have the ability to be satisfied where we are. We can use what's contained within the boundaries of a tiny front yard in rural Georgia to provide enough images for a lifetime of paintings or stories. We can paint for years using day-old cut flowers for models, and our paintings can teach others about the universe of human feelings. Some of us can come back again and again to ourselves and find the spark of new wisdom at each return.

On the other hand, some of us have a *need* to use the restless energy of a feckless wanderer's soul to roam the roads and waters of the world in service of our individual visions. The desire to know "the other side of the mountain" is a hunger some of us have and would sacrifice much to keep, even at the price of never quite knowing where "home" is and eating up precious time in transit to some unknown destination.

About ourselves, there are no visions as true as our own. Even with the myriad distortions and evasions and blind spots and ignorances we all practice in getting ourselves through life, we are who we are, and we feel the way we feel. We may argue with each other about whose vision of each other is truest, but if ever there was an ultimately absurd debate, that must be it.

In the end, the familiarity we have with ourselves is our only comfort, whether we stay close to home or wander far. It is a comfort because it is also a tool. And we need tools to work with, for until our dying breaths, we are works in progress.

▲ THE TRANCES OF INFANCY

I am indebted to Richard Shane, a therapist in Boulder, Colorado, for the idea that one's personality is a trance. It's Halloween night as I write this, the one time of year when many of us give ourselves permission to alter these personality trances, at least for a little while. Nine-year-old penguins, goblins, and ghosts are vying for elbow room on our front porch with forty-five-year-old space aliens who are late for rounds at the hospital.

Halloween is an ironically creative event, coming as it does in the trailing weeks of harvest season and setting a macabre but festive tone for the advent of winter. Little kids and adults alike perform what for many of us is the most aesthetically creative act we will do all year, when we Design Our Costumes. We allow ourselves to take on alter egos, bring hidden parts of ourselves out for others to see, and take on the identities of Boogie Men we secretly still fear on other nights of the year.

But on Halloween, we own the night. Fake fear takes the place of real fear. We willingly surround ourselves with terrifying images, and march confidently from door to door throughout our neighborhoods knowing that we will be welcomed, even by folks we barely speak to the rest of the year.

What's going on?

We are all master hypnotists. We can convince ourselves of almost anything. Because we need to feel safe, we can convince ourselves that we are safe on even dreaded Halloween night, a pagan feast of demons and the dead. On calm, beautiful nights we can convince ourselves that by the next dawn, the world is doomed. We can convince ourselves of our omnipotence, and we can equally well convince ourselves of our utter impotence.

To ourselves, we are what we believe we are. We feel as we believe we feel. Witness in memory the children we all once were, feeling helpless and alone. Cowering in the dark, many of us were often sure beyond all doubt that our bedroom floors were covered with snakes, and beneath our beds ogres lay in hungry wait.

Our fears were real by any definition, even if the snakes and ogres were not.

Infancy and early childhood is a period in which one of our main tools for understanding the world is fantasy. It is what largely defines our internal reality, and organizes but distorts our ability to accurately perceive the outside world. It is only much later in our development as human beings that external reality serves to effectively influence our internal perceptions.

The latest thinking and research on human development suggests that from our earliest glimmerings of sentience, even before our actual births, each of us is active in attempting to organize our world into a meaningful whole. As infants, we are not passive recipients, helpless and inert—we are, in the words of Samuel Slipp, a psychoanalytic author, "active, stimulus seeking, and creative" in our efforts to make sense of life.

We go through predictable stages in our early development. Initially, we learn to distinguish between ourselves and the outside world. That seemingly simple act in fact lays the foundation for our identities, and is accomplished within the first six months of our lives. Not all succeed, and some spend lives in the confusion and chaos of an unboundaried world of autism, where the self and all things seem to remain an amalgam of undifferentiated "star stuff."

Usually by our second birthdays, we learn to distinguish between ourselves and other persons, and then between others in terms of their relative "goodness" or "badness." Failure to accomplish these learning tasks leaves many of us perpetually vulnerable to primitive, utterly bottomless feelings of deprivation and helpless anger. The term "borderline" is a clinical designation for people suffering from arrest at this stage of infantile development, and evokes a haplessly accurate image of these unfortunate folks, living on the bleak and dangerous borderline of life, chronically unhappy, raging helplessly at the emptiness they sense within.

The next general phase which most of us pass through by our third birthdays is the learning that individuals around us, as well as ourselves, can at times be both "good" and "bad." Even those we love and trust can fail us at times. And we ourselves can behave badly on occasion, while maintaining a sense of being cared for and valued by others. Those who get stuck here are unable to experience this sense of worth and approval from within, and narcissistically seek, far beyond normal needs, the constant approval and attention of others as their only means of simulating self-esteem.

With these learnings and the myriad sensory and emotional experiences that accompany them, the foundations of our personalities are largely complete even before we acquire the ability to speak. Our conscious memories seldom predate our third year, yet the indications are that we largely form and solidify our notions of who we are by the time we reach our third or fourth birthday.

Hypnosis is a familiar process to each and every one of us. It boils down to gaining access to our internal resources by relaxing conscious control of our awareness. There are many names for this condition of access: trance, an altered state of consciousness, deep relaxation, half-sleep, daydreaming, reverie. Every time we become absorbed in something, whether it is a novel, a movie, a conversation, or a thought, we are in an altered state of consciousness. Driving a car is hypnotic. So is watching a fire. Many of us are clinically "in trance" at least as often as not during an average day.

What happens in these instances?

As we let go of deliberate direction of our awareness, we become aware of our interior experiences, the sensations, feelings, perceptions, fantasies, and visions of ourselves that exist within our minds as a subtext to our every minute's conscious thought.

By allowing ourselves to become aware of these experiences, we can gain the benefit of their wide range and depth. Whether we are guided into trance by a therapist's induction or we self-induce it by simply relaxing and slipping into reverie, we gain access to a level of experience outside of consciousness. These trances can be full of visual, kinesthetic, auditory, olfactory and gustatory sensations, and invested with the same level of informativeness, intelligence and native wisdom that we enjoy consciously.

The implications are momentous. We begin, probably before birth, to hypnotize ourselves into an understanding of the world and of who we are, based on sensations that when "consciously" organized are at best fantastic distortions. Unconsciously, however, we are also gathering gut-level data that in years to come continues to exist. This data is accessible through imagination and intuition and can allow us to resourcefully modify our self-perceptions and re-create our own personalities.

This in essence is the basis of hope in psychotherapy, and the basis of "truth" in creative experience.

The creative process is a kind of trance. And imagination is simply our interior experience of the possibilities of life itself.

The work of the creative person is to provide permission for his imagination to emerge into concrete reality.

Unconsciously, from our first moments of existence, we are constantly monitoring our environment with every fiber of our being. None of the information we thus gain goes to waste. It remains with us, a resource of experience that provides the basis for what we may later call intuition or creative vision, to be applied to ourselves and to our art.

▲ Irony

A friend of mine defines irony as paradox with a twist. Webster's *New Collegiate Dictionary* speaks of irony as the often humorous play of opposites, when what is said or done is the opposite of what is expected, or where the meaning of a message is the reverse of its content. Further, irony can refer to the "feigning of ignorance in argument." Socratic education is the paradigm of this type of irony. And finally, irony can connote the apparently straightforward, simple meaning of "[being] like, or containing iron."

This is a contest. Find the ironies embedded here:

> At first the screen is white—blazingly, unrelievedly white. The camera pulls back, into focus, and moves up to a dead flat horizon far in the distance, formed by a clear, blue sky above an immensely wide, snowy steppe.
>
> Gliding slowly into the vastness, inches above the ground, the camera travels for a distance before detecting a slight, indistinct variation in the white-blue interface. Now the camera approaches the scene, a small hillock, where in a patch warmed by the ascending sun and protected from the prevailing wind, a small group of bright red and purple flowers is shooting up through the melting snow.
>
> With no hesitation the camera glides inexorably through the flowers at ground level. The screen becomes filled with flashing, violent colors, as if the viewer is plowing slowly through a thick jungle of giant flowers, effortlessly overcoming the resistance of taut stems and leaves and rich moist

earth. The camera emerges at the top of the hillock, and the vast emptiness again stretches out in all directions. The camera moves on, unimpeded, unstopping. Fade focus. Fade to white ...

It could be said that irony is almost unavoidable in human behavior and communication. And especially in art. That is, we have to work at *not* being ironic, and in most instances we will fail if we try.

This is because the world in all its subtlety is fraught with ambiguity and ambivalence. Little is ever truly black or white, and the gray areas by definition contain a little of both black and white. If art at its most powerful makes us aware of the meanings wrapped in every nuance of life, then awareness of the ironies involved is central to its success. We live thick with counterpart, counterpoint, contrast, and complementarity. When as artists we seek to communicate about life in any fashion we must soon deal with the dualities of both the subject and process in which we are engaged.

Often, art is the act of becoming aware of these dualities and expressing them as directly as possible. At times we seek to add clarity to the central irony of our subjects. Or we use it as a symbol for other, similar ironies. In the visual arts, we use visual irony in the clash of color, texture, or composition as techniques to convey our awareness of complementary meanings. In music and drama, counterpoint and dissonance, unexpected volume, tempo and rhythm serve similar purposes.

In everything we do there are cores of meaning, similar to the iron core of the world. We may not always discern them, but they are there. We seek a way to find these cores and sometimes we employ devices which indirectly indicate their existence. Like magnetic compasses in the presence of iron, these devices—art, meditation, psychotherapy, moral philosophy, theology—often merely twitch erratically when they detect the presence of these core ideas, without revealing their nature and essence. But at least—and this is *so* significant—we know then they are there.

I am a member of a generation of people who when young behaved as if convinced we were immortal, while equally convinced we would never live to see ourselves middle-aged. And today, a new group is seemingly convinced that they will live on without aging at all. We care for our parents who lived, apparently, for the good life in retirement, only to find the aches, pains, and problems we are now learning to name: Alzheimer's, cancer, heart disease, and so on. The subtlety of life is the source for irony here, and for transcendence too.

Recently, I sat next to my son at a concert as we listened to Peter, Paul, and Mary sing "Puff, the Magic Dragon." I became aware of my son singing with them, and at that moment I began to weep. I was aware of many, many things: I was alive, ecstatically alive. I was forty-one years old. I had a wife, and children. I was sitting next to a son, my son, whom I never imagined having for much of my life. At the same moment as I wept for happiness I was aware I was also crying with sorrow, in the spell of a song that speaks of dragons that "live forever, but not so little boys ...." Moreover, as we sang, Puff the Magic Dragon became, in my memory, a dark converted cargo plane with banks of miniguns on either side, flying through the humid, moonlit night, capable of spraying swarms of bullets into every square foot of acres of Vietnam, through whatever and whoever alive there lay. A real, terrible dragon.

God has his little jokes, and as I lay on the grass at the concert, I tried to appreciate the one I had become aware of. Love and obscenity often look and sound the same. The meaning alone is different.

Art is in itself ironic. It is ironic that the gestures of any puny human could possibly carry such power across time. Art cannot ever be meaningless. Inaccessible, yes; banal, yes;

uncommitted, yes; poorly executed, yes. But even then, these qualities become meaningful in themselves, meanings we dislike and seek to improve upon, or to avoid, or to vilify, according to our own perceptions.

Art can be more than ironic; it can be transcendent. Witness the timeless grace of a cathedral rising amid ruins. Witness the drawings done by battered, starving people at the limits of life in the moral hell of concentration camps, drawings before which even their monstrous captors had to flinch. Witness the audacity of any portrayal of nature in art. It is inconceivable, but true, that art can at its best amplify our understanding of the vast majesty of life itself.

Art can also fail. Irony can become raw mockery. Connections can be so obscure they are impenetrable, idiosyncratic, and serve to close out rather than engage the audience. Or the connections and contrasts in a piece can be so clumsily handled, with so little respect either for the subject, the material, or the audience involved that the work is obvious, mawkish, or sloppy. Or the work itself can be false, a kind of multiple irony or mockery of the process of art itself.

A forgery has this quality. No matter the level of skill required to conceive and render the piece in question, the ultimate lie involved is that one human is trying to pass for another. Some forgeries are "successful" in that the lie is undetected and the piece is admired in itself and associated for purposes of valuation and context with the work of a particular author or artist who had nothing to do with the piece. The forger alone knows the true extent of his or her artifice. However, he can only be known as a person who would hide, whose contempt of self or fear of failure outweighs his unique sense of place in the world. The talent is artifice, not art. While the pieces these people create can and do often stand alone as well-executed, even expressive works, they stand alone as perhaps the only true bastard children in the world, often beautiful in themselves, but living under an unseen cloud. Once their illegitimacy is perchance discovered, they are identified forever thereafter not by their intrinsic merits but by their corrupt birth.

Irony often implies humor. At times, a bitter humor, to be sure, but humor is what gets us through life without going crazy, especially if we strive to be aware of the contradictions and paradoxes contained in our everyday existence. In fact, humor is what allows us to attend to and cope with the most bitter realizations.

In the movie "Last Tango in Paris" there is a scene where a life preserver is thrown into the water ... and sinks. Allow yourself to smile. It is what will allow you to examine your own life preserver without being overwhelmed.

▲ De Kooning and The Painted Word

It is late. I have, for much of the past day, been reading the catalog for the Willem de Kooning show at the East Wing of the National Gallery. De Kooning has been one of my favorite painters for a long time.

Here is what he said about art and about himself as an artist: "Content is a glimpse of something, an encounter like a flash .... When I am slipping, I say 'Hey, this is very interesting' .... As a matter of fact, I'm really slipping most of the time into that glimpse. That is a wonderful sensation, I realize right now, to slip into this glimpse. I'm like a slipping glimpser."

As I write, I am sitting in dark incandescent splendor, watching The Learning Channel in sidelong glances, and tapping away like a banana-satisfied orangutan on our laptop computer, my feet up on our Barcalounger look-alike.

Life is good. I'm like a slipping glimpser, too.

I had a friend who used to say he wanted to "out-de Kooning de Kooning." I didn't know what he meant. We shared studios for a few years. His paintings didn't look like de Kooning's stuff—but he did paint over old canvases a lot. One of his paintings was entitled *Goddamn Middle America*. Or something like that. It had red, white, and blue as part of the underpainting, I seem to recall. Maybe it is different now. The painting, I mean.

So—de Kooning. The catalog is a great thick paving brick of a tome, even in paperback, half-filled with color plates of juicy smears and dabs and "slipping glimpses" of things de Kooning saw between his days as an illustrator for World

War II-era cigarette ads and his closeout as a painter in the eighties.

The catalog contains two essays, by David Sylvester and Richard Shiff, and is a fascinating example of criticism imitating the process it purports to explain. De Kooning—explained! De Kooning explicated, contextualized ... made tiny, at last!

Talk about juice! Talk about content! How these men could make a thick, fuliginous word muck, as thick and slippery as any pot of de Kooning flesh-pink ever was, and do it with straight faces in writing the essays published in this thing, and then paste the stuff in between pictures of Willem *avec* angst—well, it is, I say, worth the price.

When you get a chance, be sure to own this book.

I'll tell you why. The reason is—not the pictures of de Kooning's paintings—but the page or so, beginning on Page 38, by Richard Shiff, about the meaning of de Kooning's offhand sketch of a woman, on which he had his wife Elaine plant six lipsticky kisses.

Those few paragraphs, a relatively small chunk of Shiff's overall effort, are a masterpiece example of what Tom Wolfe refers to in *The Painted Word* as the reductive result of Art Theory—that "essential hormone in the mating ritual" that is Modern Art—namely, the idea that "real art is nothing but what happens in your brain."

Clearly then, de Kooning's little knockoff sketch of a grinning gal is the tiny little hip wiggle that looses a righteously impressive orgasm of brain art for Mr. Shiff. Listen to this:

> The lipstick imprints can represent Elaine de Kooning's touch, Willem de Kooning's touch (since he guided the marking), a mouth (Elaine's or anyone's), and any part of the body or anything else that, when painted, resembles a mouth. Each

> imprint also represents a kiss and, by extension, any other physical act of pressing against a resistant surface. Is Elaine de Kooning kissing the female figure that Willem de Kooning has drawn, as if to enact its fetishization by adding a sign of her being? Or is she adding red accents to his composition of black marks, intensifying the pictorial effect while covering and therefore completing the sheet? Perhaps the final kiss is meant to locate a center for the represented body, and simultaneously for its paper support; Willem tended to be conscious of both kinds of center and to conflate them ....

Conflate? Center? WhooooeeeEE! Pheew! Was it good for you?

But! Shiff is not done! He is a man's man, and a critic's critic. He, if not de Kooning, is willing to answer philosopher Susan Sontag's call for "an erotics of art" in her 1964 *Evergreen Review* essay "Against Interpretation"—by making art criticism erotic!

> Pressing one's lips against a piece of paper is an experience analogous to acts of painting and drawing .... [Ooooh!] The correspondences go beyond the tactile to the synesthetic ... [Yesss!] Because the act of kissing must draw its agent flush with the image (the object of affection), perspectival [Aahh! Gasp!] distance is temporarily suspended. This is the kind of intimacy—visual, tactile, even gustatory—that Willem de Kooning desired in his art ....

Mind you, now, this is in response to a pencil scribble not much larger than a sheet of typing paper, with a bit of kissy-face for coloring! He must have crawled home wrung out like a wet towel after dealing with the "Woman" paintings.

Bruce M. Holly

But—still more? The man is a stallion! In a footnote, no less, Shiff wraps up with power and spectacular vigor (he could probably have gone on and on, brave man)—

> The ambiguity here is a result of a creative and apparently very natural play of language for which the most relevant rhetorical term is metonymy .... Metonymy occurs when an active cause is substituted for its effect, as in regarding lipstick traces as actual lips. or a kiss .... For application of such rhetorical analysis in ways relevant to the present essay, compare my "Cezanne's Physicality: The Politics of Touch" ....

How de Kooning might love this—self-referential, obtuse, thick. He himself was a simpler, but still gorgeous, dissembler on the matter of his own art, and reportedly was quite consistent at this both in his paintings and his conversations about them.

So then, de Kooning: a man well served in his lifetime by an adulatory art world, and by criticism worthy of his work.

My Lord ... fuliginous.

Frankly, after experiencing the strange light on fleshy corners provided by de Kooning's oblates in this most juicy of catalogs, I did some research, and I have a humble suggestion to make.

Brothers and sisters, we ought to let our politicians be our art critics. Don't—please God, don't—let them be art *censors*, but there is heavy evidence that they, of us all, are best-suited to the explanatory function of criticism, to the exposition of murky processes and subliminal machinations and the creation of alternate realities.

Listen: these political luminaries could be speaking about art—they could be talking about de Kooning:

- Golda Meir—"To be or not be is not a question of

compromise. Either you be or you don't be."
- Mario Cuomo—"Have no plans, and no plans to plan."
- Harold Macmillan—"He is forever poised between a cliche and an indiscretion."

De Kooning's life work—little cliche, much indiscretion. The catalog has many tips for the struggling artist, and these boil down to the usual dicta: *do* something. Do it again. Keep on *doing something*. At some point, stop. Get another canvas. Do something again. Repeat.

Welcome to de Kooning's dance. You are doing what de Kooning did.

You are an artist.

▲ Frames of Mind

Not too long ago, I was sailing in the river off the town of St. Michaels, Maryland, after having trailered my boat over for a small boat festival. In a fluke of wind, my jib sail shifted suddenly, and it whisked my glasses overboard.

I am very nearsighted. I had brought no spare pair of glasses. For the rest of the evening, I made my way in the world as if I was in a movie shot through thick gauze. Actually, it was more like I was in an Impressionist painter's animation of the world around me, a world with no detail, only shapes and color and light.

I had come to look at boats, and so I did. However, if I wanted to see anything in focus, I had to become a human microscope, peering from inches away. I had, as a result, a kind of Georgia O'Keeffe experience with watercraft of many kinds. I must have looked quite strange to bystanders as I wandered around the waterfront like a wall-eyed, bemused loon, squatting down every so often as if I was trying to sniff the varnish on some beautiful little skiff or another.

The next day, I drove home. I felt safe, as I was able to make out moving cars and trucks and people with little difficulty, and I knew the way, so reading road signs wasn't necessary.

On the bridge across the Chesapeake Bay, vibrant shadows thrown across the roadway by the latticework of the bridge structure created an intense, almost dazzling light show for me. The metallic flash of cars passing, brake lights flickering, sun on chrome—all left a faint burning trail across my field of vision, as they would on a film exposed across time. All in all, it was pretty neat.

In the course of that ride, I learned a lot about

Essays on The Psychology of Creativity

Impressionism, Abstract Expressionism, Minimalism, and theatrical lighting design, all at sixty miles an hour. I also learned to carry spare glasses.

I have had other similar experiences of feeling like the world was a living painting around me. On another day, earlier in my life, I remember feeling like I had been dropped into a surreal landscape as I stood peering through wet, foggy glasses at the dripping forest around me, trying to hear people moving in the murk while my mind raced around trying to come up with ideas about what to do next. In my mind's eye, the gray and misty image of that dank moment hangs in my memory as a portrait of myself in a soldier's youth.

I have other memories of moments where the world was like a computer screen, of moments spent playing with my own mental fractals, those random shapes generated by a computer coming to grips with chaos theory. Sometimes I've let my mind tick over like an idling engine, playing with shape after shape, and idea after idea, turning them over and over, pushing and tugging them this way and that, changing them in any direction or dimension at the drop of a hat.

And now and again I can click into a mode where every bit of everywhere I look has the potential to be a painting. It's as if the world is a movie I'm watching, and panoramic shot or close-up, every frame of the film could be converted into a valid piece of art. These are my favorite moments.

It is a gift to see. Like the gift of fire, however, seeing intensely carries risk. It is an artist's task to see. It is an artist's commitment to respond actively to the seeing.

And it is an artist's courage to keep this commitment going, over and over again in the face of the struggle that inevitably comes of the seeing of things as they are, or appear to be at the moment. Humans are prone to sensory and emotional overload, and most of us are hard-wired with plenty of neural breaker switches that can trip almost immediately to protect us from too much awareness of the world around us. It is a very hard job at times for us to keep our senses "on," and many times we tend to become less rather than more aware at times when being alert would serve us very well indeed. Similarly, it often happens that the emotional heat built up by creative energy becomes painful, and it is only by sheer force of will that many of us can stay with a creative process long enough for it to bear fruit.

But there are also times for most of us when the struggle is pure pleasure, when seeing and responding flows and sparkles with surprise and delight, a wordless intensity that is a making of love with life. You can't beat the heat then.

I'm growing dangerously fond of the computer world, and finding it seductive beyond my ability to resist as a source of metaphors for what I think the creative process is about. I sense it is dangerous to me, because I fear, catholic soul that I am, that I will someday find that my soul is in God's cold stone truth a simple on/off switch that controls my awareness of life, and my chances of salvation are measured against the amount of time I've managed to keep it on, receiving input from the world around and within me.

I further fear I will find that my salvation is, in the end, distilled to the simple knowledge that my brief being has affected others in some way. I'd have to really rework a world view then, that up to now has been quite comfortable. And like most of my phylum, I do so hate such sweeping changes.

Still, sometimes when I'm feeling frisky, I shut my eyes and play with the patterns and images I find in the darkness behind my eyelids. I'm looking for shapes yet unmade, colors yet unseen, and patterns not yet unfolded to the light of human imagination.

Won't you join me?

▲ Roaming in High Ozone

Inept as a person, Vincent Van Gogh was as clear as a bell about the structure of his art, and as innocent as a pure nun about its purpose. As a result, I believe, many of us respond to his work like hungry men respond to warm bread. There is a visual and kinesthetic accuracy about his art, and an abundance of personal emotion which informs the viewer as much about the painter as about the scene. That, I say, is my kind of art. When I look at his pictures, I feel like I'm having a conversation with a brother about ... you know, important stuff. I feel connected.

When I look at Andy Warhol's work, on the other hand, I feel a quiet, saddening distance in the conversation that takes place, which some people might say is closer to the reality that exists between most of us as human beings. Most of us seem to spend a lot of time with each other avoiding talking about "important stuff." And in quiet moments, when we become aware of this fact, the world does often seem a sad collection of surfaces, some bright and shiny, some dull as dishwater.

If both Van Gogh and Warhol were my actual brothers, I'd like Vincent better. But I'd probably hang out with Andy more. He seemed to have such good parties, and he'd be less demanding of me.

Watching old Warhol interviews seems like a way to experience one person's efforts to achieve a Zen of emotional detachment—but even this effort was, it is likely, an elaborate façade, the work of an artist using himself as both brush and canvas to embody the meaning, look, and feel of—loneliness.

Harry Stack Sullivan, during the early and mid-twentieth century, created a framework for psychiatry which emphasizes the interpersonal social influences which drive human development. In his view, it takes a comparatively long time—from infancy almost until pre-adolescence—for most of us to develop the capacity to be truly lonely, or in his words, to collect "the components which culminate in the experience of real loneliness ... the need for contact ... the need for acceptance ... the need for intimate exchange with a fellow being ...."

Sullivan further postulated that "validation of personal worth requires ... collaboration." In other words, we need each other to establish our personal meaning in the universe and to validate our creative choices in life.

I've occasionally had the fantasy that there would be much less pain attached to living this complex existence if we could live without feeling—if we could be absolutely without sentiment about ourselves, each other, our activities, possessions, and so on. Some say animals enjoy this kind of freedom from the pain of emotion. But even most animals seem bound to some form of instinctual loyalty or "caring." The level of detachment I'm speaking of seems to exist in nature only at the level of insects or primordial creatures such as worms and bacteria.

There are people who give us a glimpse of life without emotional connection. Autistic individuals live a life characterized by this lack. But the most frightening humans alive are those of us who are missing what Jerome Kagan, a social psychologist at Harvard University, refers to as "moral emotions"—anxiety, fear, and guilt. These are the sociopaths, some of whom are the most heartless of human criminals, liars, and users who live a self-contained, emotionally painless life, victims of a mental illness that robs them of the privilege of loneliness, or empathy. And without empathy, they often embody human evil. Their lack of pain and loss makes the fantasy of emotional invulnerability an ugly reality.

There are times when I find myself staring at piles of

bubbles—for instance, the kind you get in a sink with soapy dishwater. The kaleidoscope of images reflected on their surfaces is fascinating; the temporary fragility of thousands of shimmering, ephemeral surfaces in constant flux seems so mysterious, so random, so vastly complex as to be impossible to understand. But it isn't.

Each bubble has a surface completely subservient to known laws of physics. Each bubble depends on neighboring bubbles for its own unique shape. Temperature, movement, subtle gravitational forces—all play their part in making the mix what it is. Given the circumstances that obtain at any given moment, the sinkful of millions of bubbles could look no different than it does.

Extrapolating a bit, there are similar explicable reasons for every occurrence, at every step of the way through our lives. There are occasions when things seem accidental, but with a broad enough focus, there are enough discernable influences to make what we do inevitable.

What I am proposing here is that there are no isolated, random occurrences in any sphere of our universe. There are, as Sigmund Freud suggested about the human psyche, no accidents. At the outset, please note that what I'm saying has a tight focus on the natural universe. God knows what else there is going on, but for the purposes of this essay, I don't.

So what? Here are some implications:

- Life is infinitely more complex than we can imagine. Simplicity does not exist.
- Nothing exists in isolation.
- There is no such thing as meaninglessness.

At the moment of the birth of the universe, we, our present world, indeed the next thoughts you have, were made inevitable. We, in our entirety—bodies, minds, and arguably souls—are agglomerations of star stuff set in motion eons ago, chemicals which at this particular moment in time are interacting in relationships which result in muscle and bone, and thought—and feeling. Time, moreover, is a mutable illusion, a function of the constant change in these relationships.

What is the point of all this? How do notions of human loneliness relate to the notion that choice is an illusion? Further, what does the fantasy of a life lived without feeling have to do with either loneliness or illusion? What do these veerings signify for the creative process?

The notion of life without feeling is clearly an impossibility in the midst of an immense unseen swell of causal influences on every aspect of our thoughts, perceptions, and behavior. Living is feeling. Emotion is an energy as inevitable as heat or light. And it is the essence of creativity.

Most of us have the capacity to feel lonely when we deal with life without benefit of contact with our fellows. Through loneliness, we become aware of a need, deeper than a hunger, for validation by other human beings. We are then motivated by this need, this feeling, this intangible, real energy—to create, beyond our animal existence, some form of intimate connection with our brothers and sisters.

Creativity depends on choice. It is an activity of human beings working in the present. As human beings, we live in blissful ignorance of the next moment. As far as we are concerned, we have a variety of possibilities available. Our limited perception of what is going on gives us the illusion of wide-open choice.

But unbeknownst to us, in the moment that is now, we respond in the only way possible to our motivating emotions and perceptions, given the myriad factors that have been converging on this instant since the beginning of time.

There is this to know, then: when we create, we do so because we are conformed to do so at the moment, and we desire to create because we have no alternative. As the stars could be in no other order at this point in time, we could do no other.

At this instant, this is the only of all possible worlds.

▲ THE MEANING OF MEANING: AN INITIAL SALLY AND RANDOM THOUGHTS

I'm not sure who said "What God thinks, is." But I do know that there have always been people who would say in response "Is it? Is what? What's God? Why? Whaat?"

"Meaning" is one of those words that you understand until you're asked to define it. After a pause, most of us will come up with words that match the dictionary's definition fairly closely: "The intent, aim, or object of a statement or action ... the sense in which a statement is understood ... the significance or import of a thing or activity." To mean something is to "... intend or wish" it, or to "have in mind a purpose or an object ... a reference or a destination."

"To have in mind ..." I think we're on to something here. By these definitions, meaning is a consciously developed characteristic.

But most of us do a lot of apparently "mindless" things. Daily, most of us say things which, in terms of carrying a specific message to someone else, amount to gibberish. Some of us specialize in such statements. In fact, it is precisely to avoid or disguise what we have in mind that we say a lot of things.

Both the sender and the receiver of a message assign meaning to it. Whose meaning is most valid, if they differ? In the end, can anything really mean everything? Have politicians and pundits been right all along? Do messages mean what you want them to mean, regardless of what the sender intended? Is there any such thing as absolute meaning, where "no" really means "no," and "never" and "forever" have no options available? Is "maybe" the most absolute thing a human being can say this side of a leap of faith?

Absolute freedom brings absolute absurdity to many aspects of human life, and this is one of them. If we had no sense that the maker of a message has both responsibility and prerogative to intend something specific, most of our conversation would sound like bad off-Broadway. But the fact is, and it is at times a scary fact, that we sometimes do intend things we are not conscious of, and our audience picks up on these things accurately. Or the meanings assigned to a message by persons other than the maker are more cogent or useful or accurate than the originator's intent.

The reality that humans can get anything across to each other that means roughly the same thing for both sender and receiver is evidence of a raw, positive power of judgment and flexibility that we will never fully understand—it suggests that as a race we are gifted with an intelligence far beyond our capacity to use fully.

Oh, Lord, what corridors of freedom and ambiguity this opens up, particularly in the arts. Meaning in art has so many visible facets, and exists in so many forms, that artist and critic alike often stagger around like stupefied drunks in a mirror maze trying to describe it, confused by all the possibilities.

So what? So it boils down to this—understanding the "what" and the "why" of our lives, and conveying this understanding to others so they can understand us, are needs as deep as hunger or sex, and they are as powerful as hunger in motivating our behavior. But we can never be satisfied in these needs, because in the end, meaning—the significance within each and every human act—is so complex that the best we do is catch or convey only part of it intentionally, and the parts we intuitively comprehend vary with every passing second.

Viktor Frankl, a Viennese psychiatrist, built a theory and technique of psychotherapy in the 1930's and 40's on the notion that man lives for meaning. Then, he refined his theory in a personal cauldron of pain as one of millions of people who in the Holocaust became a burnt offering to a God who seemed to have vacated the universe at the time. In *Man's Search For Meaning*, Frankl speaks of the importance of discovering and grasping the essential significance available in even absurd events that allows one to survive, and in doing so, to surmount life itself. I remember that at first reading, and then for years after, what Frankl wrote *about* meaning made no real sense to me. But what his descriptions of his own personal hell on earth in Auschwitz did was give me a glimmer of a feeling that even in hell, there is the possibility of finding an answer to the question: "What is the meaning of this for *me*?"

An answer is not *the* answer. But it's a start, and given who and what we are, without the revelation of divine tidings, it's the best we can do. For Frankl, it seemed that the preservation of his ability to pay homage to his wife's memory is what kept him going. It gave him a core reason for continuing to live. And at the same moment, around him thousands of other suffering souls were likewise struggling through each moment, fueled by their own reasons to survive.

In the end, in life and in art, meaning is an intensely personal aspect of our experience. We each come up with our own.

At about the same time that I was reading Frankl's work, I was developing an image about what my purpose in life was. I've told you about it before, but here it is again: someday, as I am walking down a street after a rainstorm, my shadow slides across a rain puddle, momentarily blocking the glare of reflected sunlight so that it fails to blind a passing truck driver. As a result, he is able to see and avoid a young woman with a baby carriage crossing the street in front of him. Years later, the infant in the carriage grows up to become the great great grandmother of the architect of lasting world peace. I will have existed to cast that shadow, at that moment.

Why do I live and work? In a sense, it is a compelling need to be here when the time comes to cast my shadow.

Early one morning earlier this year, I left my home in northern Virginia on a motorcycle with forty-eight hours on my hands and no clear destination. Several hours later, I was rolling over hill and hollow on the Blue Ridge Parkway in western Virginia, filled to the point of ecstasy with the warm smells of a ripening mountain springtime. Then I turned east on a whim toward Lynchburg, with a half-serious idea that I might run into Jerry Falwell. No luck, though I drove around town for some time. I headed further east, through peanut country, and ended up in late afternoon with ten dollars in my wallet and a ten-dollar toll in front of me if I wanted to cross the twenty-two-mile Chesapeake Bay Bridge Tunnel from Norfolk to the Eastern Shore of Virginia at the mouth of the Bay.

Or I could head home.

An hour later, I found myself racing across the last few feet of bridge, with empty pockets and a feeling of edgy commitment to a project that made no sense. I was going to circumnavigate the Chesapeake Bay for the pure heck of it. I felt twenty years younger and not one bit foolish.

The day had started gray and cool in the mountains. Now, roaring through the salt air with beach sand in every direction, I was comfortable in a T-shirt at seventy miles an hour. A destination was forming, still a hundred miles down the road—my friends' home on a marsh island near Crisfield, Maryland.

My friends were going out for the evening. I wasn't ready to stop, anyway. With a ten-dollar loan, I could look forward to a meal. Onward!

Bruce M. Holly

    Finally, it was time to call it a day, and I ran through deepening evening and a rain shower toward the Atlantic and my brother and sister-in-law's beach apartment in Ocean City, Maryland. As I pulled in behind their place, I began my six hundredth mile of the day. I had no idea what my purpose was for the effort, and no good sense of the meaning for me in the overall scheme of things. I just knew it was important to me to be doing it. I also had little feeling below my navel.

    My brother was impressed. He understands conceptual art.

▲ Beyond Memory

In his autobiography *Memories, Dreams and Reflections*, Carl Jung decided to describe his life by largely dismissing the people and events he encountered as essentially unimportant in understanding him as a person. As a prologue to his story, he wrote, "I have now undertaken ... to tell my personal myth .... Whether or not the stories are 'true' is not my problem. The only question is whether what I tell is *my* fable, *my* truth."

For Jung, the meaningful action in his life, the stuff worth preserving for others, happened between his ears. In his words, "I can understand myself only in light of inner happenings. It is these that make up the singularity of my life, and with these my autobiography deals."

What is a memory? On the biological plane, memory is a function of our brains' capacities to store information in particular configurations of nerves and unique chemical sequences that occur in myriad folds and undulations of cerebral tissue. In physical terms, a memory is a millisecond's worth of electrical discharge, nothing more.

In terms of human importance, however, memory is the building material of the human mind. One's memories define what one's life has been, and shape one's expectations for tomorrow. And memories shared with other human beings often take on additional power: the power to deepen intimacy, the power to correct distortions and give consensus to history, and the potential to heal past pain by examining it in a safe and caring present context.

Memory is getting a lot of attention in science and society these days. We're learning more each day, for instance, about the ravages of Alzheimer's Disease, a condition many of us face as we get older. One of the saddest and most painful aspects of Alzheimer's is a loss of memory so profound that in the end, even the names of our own children flee from recall, a loss often more difficult for patient and family to cope with than loss of limb or sight or hearing, because in a very real way it is a loss of one's very self, forever.

On another front, the recovery of memories of past abuse which many of us experience is under question in many courts. Are these memories real? Do they accurately document actual events so painful we put them out of mind, often for years, before they bubble again to the surface of our consciousness? Or are they imaginary constructions made from suggestions or in response to thoughts and fears of what *might* have happened? The earnestness with which well-intentioned and conscientious individuals debate this issue illustrates the importance and the complexity of memory as a part of our experience of life. Here especially, whatever the legally recognized facts of what happened at a given time in the past, the significance of one's *perception* of reality if undeniable.

The arts, all of them, rely on an accumulation of human experience, perceived uniquely by individual artists. Each of us contributes to this accumulation by our creative work, which unavoidably is shaped by every firing of every synapse we have ever owned since Poppa's sperm arrived at Momma's egg. The original record of most, if not all, of these events exists in our minds as memory.

Art is a means of sharing memory, of expressing one's emotional and historical past in a way meaningful far beyond the simple recounting of the physical facts of one's life. Creative art makes tangible the often wordless music of the human mind, a music composed of phrases and grace notes found only in our deepest personal archaeologies. Additionally, art contributes to the development of a shared societal language about human experience which is part and parcel of the "collective unconscious" that Jung referred to in his theoretical writings.

In this way, art provides a kind of race memory of humankind and a language for describing it. As our individual pasts beget our collective futures, so our individual creative perceptions beget our collective creative expression.

Most of us date our earliest recoverable memories back to when we were three or four years of age. Often these recollections are fleeting experiences of a scene or an object, or a smell, texture, or sound ingrained in our psyches from early on, and powerful enough even in trace amounts to bridge the passing of years.

My earliest memory is of a green-and-white rectangular can of olive oil. It is a flash of an image which, if I work at it, I can hold in my mind's eye and focus, as you might do with a slide projector. The top half of the can was a glossy bone white, and the lower half a medium-dark forest green. The cap on top, a screw-on that I had trouble turning by myself, was in a corner of the can, and I can't quite recall what the lettering on the can said, or where it was placed.

I can recall the special taste of the oil inside, when our housekeeper poured it over bread with slices of onion on top. We lived in Greece at the time and I was about three years old.

I have another memory—my first experience of myself as an artist in the first grade. By then we were living in France. I drew an elaborate ocean liner, a "Queen Elizabeth" or "S.S. United States" type of ship, passing a shoreline filled with skyscrapers—the New York of my young imagination. The ship had a word written on its dark hull, because it was drawn as an exercise to illustrate some rule of grammar, as I recall. I remember being very proud of my drawing, and I remember feeling both pleased and puzzled when my mother had it framed and hung it up. I felt like the word on the ship was too intrusive to make it worth framing.

Bruce M. Holly

For the next four decades, my mother hung that picture up in every apartment and house where our family lived. I still feel the same pride and puzzlement when I look at it. The word on the ship's hull still sticks out and disturbs me.

In that memory alone, I recognize themes and attitudes which continue to color my work today and my responses to the creative work of others. At age six I was embarked on a voyage which oscillated uncomfortably between the practical and the sublime. I recognize now the discomfort over using the picture as a vehicle to learn grammar: in my young mind, I was grappling with the distinction between commercial and fine art, and I hadn't yet learned that the distinction might well be a false one.

I think I'll go have an onion and olive oil sandwich. Want one?

▲ Wandering Among Ideas

When I set out to write this essay, I had a fair idea of what I wanted to write about: ideas. What they are, where they come from, how they manifest themselves to us, and how we use them. It seemed a fine project until I tried to write things down. Almost immediately, I lost focus. I lost direction. I censored my ideas about ideas as too obvious or too fuzzy before I even completed my thoughts, much less committed them to paper.

And so, I cast about. I needed something specific to write about in the worst way.

Originally, I had thought of writing about some of the observations about children's art I had come across in an article by Ellen Winner, a psychologist with Project Zero at Harvard University. In the article, research is cited indicating that children even as young as two years of age are attempting to purposefully represent their experiences in their scribbles. Gesturally as well as pictorially a child's drawings are, according to Winner, the "glimmerings of the idea that marks on a page can stand for things in the world."

Describing how children proceed developmentally in art, Dr. Winner cites a variety of research with various hypotheses about why children draw the way they do. For instance, she notes that "artistic" children characteristically demonstrate more visual-memory skill than children who are not artistically productive. They remember more visual detail about their subjects, and put it into their drawings. According to Dr. Winner, "Apparently, children with drawing talent simply cannot forget the patterns they see around them, just as musicians often report being unable to get melodies out of their minds."

Children, like adults, attempt to simplify and select elements in attempting to represent them. They do it freely and with few limits, responding to their own interests in the subject matter. As they grow, they typically develop more investment in "realism" in their work and are increasingly able to draw out the increased detail, perspective, and differentiation that characterizes most people's work at later developmental stages.

However, this growing investment in "getting things right" also exposes the developing artist to the risks of becoming enslaved to a particular "right" way to see and draw. While this stage opens the door to growing technical competence, for many young artists it is also the stage at which many abandon artistic activity as too hard or internalize so many rules about what is correct or incorrect that their artwork loses life while gaining accuracy.

At the end of her article, Dr. Winner quotes Picasso's statement "I used to draw like Raphael, but it has taken me a whole lifetime to learn to draw like children."

I couldn't seem to maintain interest in responding to the article. Much as I wanted to, much as I could see that it applied to a discussion about ideas, I couldn't stay with any thought long enough to write it down.

In a fit of absent-minded desperation, I picked up an English translation of psychologist Jean Piaget's *Play, Dreams, and Imitation in Childhood*. After a brief bout, Piaget's prose—dense, involuted, referential—won handily over my ability to concentrate. I was left, however, with a phrase: "the joy of being the cause." And a thought: in criticizing another psychologist's theory of what play is, Piaget reviews the notion that in children's play, "The pleasure of being the cause reminds us that it is we who are creating the illusion. This is why play is accompanied by a feeling of freedom and is the herald of art, which is the full flowering of this spontaneous creation."

I stopped with the thought. It seemed to ring true for me. There is a "joy in being the cause" of something's existence, whether it is a thought, an action, an artwork, or a person. It is as close to being as free and God-like as we can humanly come. But for the joy to come, the work of causation has to begin.

Moreover, it can be a fragile joy, if we allow ourselves to be aware of the uncounted times others have thought, done, or made things similar to our efforts. Some of us struggle with the illusion that there is nothing really new under the sun. At worst, we accept it as a truth. As a result, we discount and discard our own efforts as redundant, irrelevant, or insignificant.

What we also tend to discount is that we are only aware of the thoughts and actions of those people who choose to do something to communicate them. And they, in the vast scheme of things, are a minuscule minority of the population, made unique among their peers by their actions.

I wandered into town and walked into a bookstore, for want of anything better to do. I was frustrated, out of sorts, and felt tied up tight. It's a feeling familiar to me when I go into art galleries too, sometimes.

Sometimes, being exposed to the concrete reality of books, paintings, and sculpture that others have done stimulates me to unbind myself. Sometimes—less often, thank God—I'm intensified in my stuckness, and leave a bookstore or gallery with an empty sense of banality about my own work and most everyone else's. There's a certain unpredictability about which effect will occur, and I often feel that going into these places is a bit of a dice roll.

On this occasion I spent a lot of time in the cheap book section, the area where they sell books for a buck or so. People give their ideas a shot, and then they end up in disheveled stacks, cloaked in anonymity, victims of poor sales. I've bought a number of good books there. Sometimes, I even get the message that these ideas count too.

I walked up and down each aisle, sometimes looking for a particular book or author as if for an old friend. I passed the Impressionists, into the food section, through the mysteries, into the children's area. I sneaked peeks into sexy books like a guilty kid and wondered how many others had done so. I became aware again of a thought I'd had in different guises before: I was walking past and through a vast pile of accumulated knowledge that could be mine. All that was needed was for me to attend to it. That's what a bookstore is for me—a dream world of real knowledge.

Dreams are, according to Freud, the images of our fulfilled wishes—displaced, distorted, and disguised—the products of our minds unfettered by limits of reality or conscience. At the heart of it, they can be seen as our efforts to recover the basic security and well-being of an ideal childhood.

Others, more recently, have looked at dreams as the sputterings and misfirings of nerve endings and leftover sensory images which our brains, not fully out of gear even in sleep, attempt to organize.

In either case, our dreams are significant, as significant as the play and art of children, as significant as our half-unconscious meanderings through a life filled with patterns, messages, and meanings. Either as messages in themselves or as stimuli for us to form meanings, these experiences give us the potential for expression of ourselves and for connection with our fellow humans.

John Rosenthal, a poet, recently noted, "You don't write poems when you live in Eden—you write poems when you've left and you can't find your way back." I know the feeling.

▲ THE MOMENT IS NOW

"You can do anything you have to."
—Terry Anderson,
American hostage, released after seven years of
captivity in Lebanon, 1992.

Early on, I saw this essay in my mind, flowing like easy water off the end of my pen, flowing with no pause, pressure-fed by the feelings I had (and have) in watching my closest friend and his wife cope with the news that their son is seriously ill.

It's not coming out that way, though.

My godson. This is too close—the fear that comes when bad things happen to people I know and love. This is the kind of pain that we watch on the ll o'clock news, for God's sake, cameras tight on the faces of anguished strangers, not ... *us*.

It's so hard to make sense of what begs for accurate expression—this is life at its most ragged, after all. How strange and muted, how unreal, and how mundane are the settings for such pain—the dull, deserted hospital hall used as a waiting area for families with children in surgery, the answering machines that mark the terminus of phone calls to parents fully absorbed in the rising and falling of their unconscious child's breast, the faceless tones of a doctor breaking news to a frightened couple struggling for composure, or numbness, whichever comes first.

There is ultimately no escape from the truth here—life is unpredictable for each and every one of us, and it is *so* frail. My godson included, we all live day to day, and beyond the moment, and I mean right *now*, nothing more is ever guaranteed, our ever-present fantasies notwithstanding. There is no tomorrow. Now is all there is.

It's so easy to say this is wisdom when the life on the line is someone else's son. My heart screams for my friends, and I'm fighting a hard battle for the courage to even stay close to them in their own pain and fear. It's beyond my ability to fathom what they are actually experiencing.

We create with each moment of our lives, by simply weaving together the little things that allow us to see what this instant becomes. Creativity is occasionally nothing more than the mere endurance of an inescapable moment. Survival is the act that allows the future to unfold.

My godson is hard at work, now, weaving. So are his folks. Each of us is bringing the thread of every past moment in our lives to the time at hand. Every subtle permutation of meaning in these personal tapestries vies against the soft constant pressure of unraveling despair that wells up in such dark hours. In these moments, the meaning of all of this is so hard to see. The shape of things to come is indistinct, and in the looming ether of the next instant, truths once clear fade in and out like the broken brushstrokes of a confused and overladen landscape.

Serious illness in a child demands the wildest, most desperate efforts at abstraction in an onlooker. There is no balancing logic, no fairness, no tradition to draw on for understanding. There is no schooling for competence in watching the suffering of a youngster. Parents, friends, the world at large, all must invent their own theories of why and how such a travesty occurs in nature.

The colors of a pediatric ward do not complement each other—the primary reds and blues and yellows of children's art are not well-framed by the smudgy-steel glint of hospital fixtures. They war with each other. They do not belong in the same universe with each other. And yet, in human terms, they are among the most complementary of symbols for what goes on in such a place, for the healing that is so often the result of going through hell.

My friends are as if in prison now on such a ward, in a hell every parent dreads. And their son is bound to his own personal moment at the edge of what comes.

I want so much for things to be okay for my friends. Wishing and wanting don't make reality, but they give direction to our hopes. And my hope of this moment is that the life of this child is full and good.

It is hard to stay with them through this time. But it is impossible not to. It would be like turning away from creation itself.

There is something familiar to me in what is happening. I've been here before. I am a spectator in an event that is so acutely powerful that it hurts even to watch. On another level, I am deeply involved. These are my friends, and I can withdraw from them only at the cost of my self-respect. They need me, and I *want* them to need me. On the other hand, I want not to have to deal with what's happening so bad I can taste it. It really is like a dream, a nightmare, but one that I can escape only by becoming unconscious. My best guess is that these are similar to my friends' feelings, but for them, the feelings are likely far more intense and far more complex.

What's familiar about this is that I feel this way when I do art. My artwork comes hard, and happens only when I have the courage to express my witness of things within myself that are far from safe, and as illogical and often brutal as the illness of a child. Truth be told, I avoid my own artwork, process and product, as often as I try to avoid facing the awareness, day to day, that suffering is a common, rather than unusual, human experience.

At the beginning of a work, nothing is guaranteed. Everything is an effort, and the early news is often bad about where things look like they are going. Sometimes, the work takes a lot of grinding effort, for a long, long time. And often, it ends up far, far different in the end than what I intended in the beginning. Sometimes, the result is clearly worth the effort. More often, it's not so clear.

Much like the situation my godson is in.

For me, the two processes are comparable, and in making the comparison, neither is trivialized. I wish I had not learned of this comparison, but I have. That it seems apt makes the present no less painful.

There is no tomorrow. There is only, and forever, only *now*, a moment that includes the hope of a better time to come. My friends' child lives. He is alive now. He eats, and breathes, and cries, and laughs. What comes next is—he is alive, *now*. That is the future. That is now.

For me right this moment, that attitude makes for better enduring, and in other moments, for better art.

▲ Time

Time is a commodity. It is a state of mind. And it is a framework. It serves as a way of dividing up our experience into pieces that we can discuss, and ordering the discussion so we can keep things straight. It has one of the longest definitions in the English dictionary. Look it up. There is no creative act of man that fails to involve the concept of time in some fashion. It is ubiquitous.

We often describe time by personifying it as if it were a living being: time flies from us when we're having fun, and catches up to us when we're fooling around. Time is an inexorable monster, moving toward us like a Leviathan. Sometimes, we treat it as a thing which can be possessed: we have time, we find a few hours, we keep time available. We lose time all over the place, and pieces of time must surely be strewn everywhere somewhere. Time is like a river, ever the same, ever changing. It flows, grinds, lurches, crawls, leaps, marches, and springs.

Other images of time as a commodity abound. Time is precious, and it can be stolen. Once lost, it can never be recovered. Occasionally, it can be bought, usually at a high price.

And yet, elusive as it is, the moment we are in lasts forever. With this notion, time becomes a state of mind.

Man is the only being to be able to transcend time, to alter the perceptions that lock most sentient creatures firmly into the present. Using self-hypnosis, many people can deliberately achieve the ability to distort their perception of the passage of time. Minutes feel like hours, hours feel like minutes. Actually, with less deliberate control, this is a fairly common and familiar experience for most people. Who has not felt the hours before dawn that seem to stretch into eternity? Who has not been surprised by the end of an all-too-brief vacation?

In situations where our concentration and focus are riveted on the passage of time, especially as we move toward a goal, it seems to stretch. In a sense, we get an opportunity to witness the movement of the present into the past without distraction. As that is what we are attending, we become exquisitely aware of each and every nuance of the anticipatory feelings and anxiety which usually are present.

On the other hand, when our full focus is on an experience rather than on the process of time—on the feelings, sensations, and complexities of the immediate moment—time seems to pass from our awareness. The present is forever, until we break concentration and notice that the world around us has moved on, and the clock with it.

Man is also perhaps the only sentient being capable of imprisoning himself in the past. Memory is our doorway to the past, and the memories may be conscious, unconscious, or embedded in our senses, where they are more commonly referred to as intuitions. And like most doorways, this one swings open or closed to us depending on the exigencies of the moment. The feelings and, often, the behavior sparked by our memories are as real today as when they first appeared in our lives.

Moreover, we often respond to people in the present as if they were similar to, or the same as, the people in our past who first gave rise to these feelings. These are common human responses to a need to make things familiar. Carried to extremes, however, these tendencies can lead to pathologically inappropriate ways of treating all members of a class: all men become seen as unreliable as one's alcoholic father, all women as needy and demanding as one's narcissistic mother, and so on.

For some, memories become the reality of the moment,

and the door slams shut on the present. The sad people populating our city streets, muttering to unseen enemies and lovers as they search through garbage, may offer us visions of what this is like.

Imagination is another gateway in the fabric of time for humans. Imagination allows us access to past events beyond record, and most especially, it opens the future to us. And as with memory, it swings both ways for most of us, depending on our needs and capacities. Anticipation may serve as an incentive for change and an encouragement to move on, or it can serve as a foretaste of doom, a promise of hell to come. And for some, fear of the future becomes the process that defines their lives in various guises.

The pessimists among us use imagination to scan the future for the worst possible scenario. The optimists visualize the best possible turnout ahead, and move forward in high hopes.

The wise in both groups prepare similarly for whatever the future brings. They know two things: imagination is fallible, and the cosmos really does have its random moments.

Finally, time is a framework, a cosmic armature which orders chaos, separates causes from effects, and provides the environment for what we call meaning to emerge from events which seem essentially unrelated. This seems to apply both on a cosmic level, and on a personal level. Time is the dimension that allows for movement and change in all things. Time does not teach, but it allows for learning.

I occasionally guide artists through a particular form of self-critique. It is a very personal experience, and involves elements of both aesthetic critique and personal psychotherapy.

In this process, we begin by spending some time developing a factual and emotional history of the artist's life to date. This is done through my interviewing the artist about specific periods in his or her life, by our gathering information from family sources such as scrapbooks and photographs, and by arranging this information along a personal time line, similar to those constructed by high school students studying world history.

We also construct a genogram, a device often used in family therapy to discover family relationships that sometimes transcend generations. Basically, a genogram is a carefully-constructed, complete family tree, which contains the basic facts of life: birthdates, deathdates, names, and so on. However, a genogram goes further than a family tree, and includes information about the emotional meaning of each member of the family for the subject, and about the relationships which exist or have existed between each family member. Intimate details of the family's history can come to light during this process, and in so doing, the emotional impact of events can be studied, such as the leaving home by one sibling, the death of a parent, the importance of a particularly influential grandmother, and so on.

Following this part of the process, the artist selects personal artworks to examine from the perspective of the events in his or her personal history, and the information and insights he or she may have gained in developing the time lines and genograms. Some choose to review their entire body of work, including works done during their childhoods, until the present day. Others are particularly interested in examining a specific phase of their work, or a particular set of elements or symbols in the work they are doing. In any case, the focus can be as broad or as narrow as necessary to serve the artist at the moment.

In the process of self-critique, one's own art can serve a purpose unavailable to most people: as artists we have a record of our emotional, often unconscious lives which can provide us with images of ourselves far more deep and true than any photograph. Art becomes, for the artist/author, a means of transcending that elusive commodity, that state of mind, time itself, while using it as a means of gaining deeper personal knowledge.

Time passes with each beat of every human heart. But each moment which enters the past becomes a reality for all eternity. Art is a particularly potent form of describing that reality—and of keeping it available in times to come.

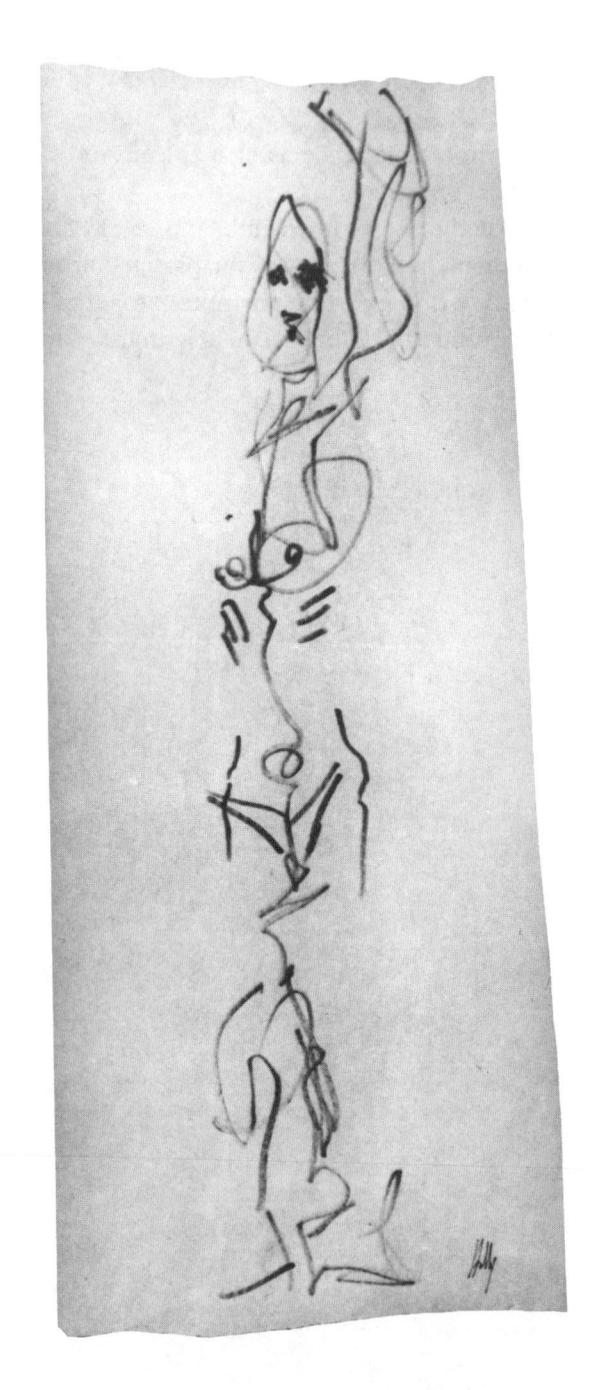

Chalk on Paper,
36"x12", ©1983, Bruce Holly

▲ Exposure

Once upon a time, I did some modeling in the nude. A bunch of us worked together in a studio, and modeled for each other, usually with clothes on. One evening, out of curiosity, I decided to take it all off, and see what that was like.

Wow.

Exposing oneself is a loaded act, loaded with emotion, meaning, and risk. Exposing one's experience of the world is similarly freighted, for one's self and one's experience are interlocked so tightly as to be inseparable.

Art is exposure—if not of the artist then of the artist's world. Art is the result of someone acting creatively on his or her experience. In a sense, artists are their art.

But, conversely, to say that art is the artist—that is, that art serves to reveal the artist completely—is in a lunatic way the same as saying a glass of water is a river.

Art is often noble, timeless, and elegant in its elemental power, but in itself is evidence of only a portion of one person's experience at one specific moment in time. It is at best a mere chip of the mountain of unique life each of us stands atop, a mountain which often changes radically from instant to instant. Art represents and communicates only the portion of our experience which catches our attention and interest in a given moment, and while we may think we are choosing the jewels of the minute, it may only be because we fail to see deeper into the heart of the hill beneath us. Or because we only focus on the nuggets which require the least work to capture, or choose to chase after elusive, half-glimpsed veins of precious ore, we thus miss the equally valuable and easier pickings at our feet.

Moreover, we may choose pieces of our personal mountains which fascinate us, but fail to capture the interest of others—expressed in art, these are the works which may be of value in understanding the artist, but in themselves fail to touch the viewer personally, and thus fail as art which stands alone.

The point is, as much as we show of ourselves in art or otherwise, there's always more, and maybe better, left untouched.

We need ways of encouraging and consoling ourselves as we go through the process of exposure in art—at least it seems most of us do—for exposure is at once one of the most feared and desired of human conditions.

Exposure involves being known, and it involves being willing to know. It allows us to be seen and recognized for what we are, at the risk of being rejected for what we are. It involves being in the presence of risk in order to know what life is fully like.

The risk of the drop is the price of knowing what the abyss is about. By avoiding risk, we may feel safe, but only in the sense that a prisoner left unattended in a dark cell can feel safe, in that for the moment, we experience no harm. But then we are wasted by the slow death of fear itself.

Some of us imprison ourselves with shame, the horror of our most terrible secrets becoming revealed so others will feel the same contempt for us that we do. It seems the deepest pits of hell on earth are reserved for those of us who believe that somehow, we have committed unpardonable sins. Many of us spend our lives trying to hide, alone and sickened. Standing stock still in our shame may seem safest, but we get nowhere. And meanwhile, for each of us, the clock is running out through every minute of our sad immobility.

The human truth is, by our being known, and accepted, and fully understood, we can be both healed and increased. But for many of us, doing so is as difficult as stepping out of an airplane in flight with no parachute, with no guarantee that one will be handed to us on the way down.

For each of us, our creative process develops unique characteristics which stay much the same, time after time, and become familiar and predictable to us. Sometimes, these characteristics are unpleasant or disconcerting. The kernel of good often balances against a great deal of pain in pursuing creative effort.

The process of creative exposure has a beginning, middle, and ending phase. At best (and usually), it is a cyclic process, one that renews and re-invigorates itself. And, as in most activities we do repetitively, we settle into routines that seem to help us begin, make the transitions between phases, and come to stopping points.

Moreover, these routines help us cope with the demands of the tasks in front of us, or with the drain of the phases we have accomplished. They give us a comforting sense, though it is often an illusion, that we know what to expect next. They are related to routines we learned early in life, the primitive rhythms we fell into that helped us through the basic tasks of playing, eating, and finding love. Our creative efforts are often sparked by sense-memories of how our infantile action led to satiation of these most basic needs.

Our adult need for creative expression is no less basic. Across history, artists' muses have taken a variety of forms, from the ripe, vibrant youth of beautiful women to the smell of a drawerful of rotting apples. Our routines as artists vary from elaborate readying rituals to the studied creation of chaos as a prelude to creative work; some of us require the peace and serenity of Walden Pond to get under way; others of us need the noise and grit and danger of late-night 42nd Street New York. Deadlines murder the Muse for some, while for others, she doesn't even show up until the eleventh hour has almost ticked away.

Ever since I was a young kid, I've loved to travel, most

especially alone, as much for the trip as for the destination. It seems I do my best thinking while I'm driving.

I've noticed that I go through discreet, predictable stages within myself on each and every outing.

Before I start out, I tend to minimize the difficulty and magnitude of the trip. I do this by speaking offhandedly about "a little drive" of thousands of miles, for instance. I put off planning or packing until the last minute. And inevitably, I rush myself into the journey in a blur of activity that gets me through the goodbyes and farewells that, were I to really experience them, might be enough to keep me from going away at all.

The first few miles are spent fidgeting, getting comfortable, getting things just so, until—at a certain time which varies but always comes—I am overwhelmed by what I've been avoiding. I am alone, miles from home, in unfamiliar territory, isolated in the fast lane on the way to somewhere equally unfamiliar. I'm out of touch with the people I love, and during this phase, I'm out of touch with the part of me that knows this is what I want to do. It is a miserable phase for me. I'm often flooded with feelings of guilt, abandonment, sadness, and loss. I feel small, helpless, and weak. Frankly, it hurts, often a lot.

Finally, again it seems inevitably, this flood of regret and fear passes, and is replaced, often for the rest of the journey, with a sense of serenity and confidence. At times, I think I've seen the face of God at this point. It's why I travel alone, truth be known, and cheaper and better in every way than drugs.

I relax, and sink deep into the rhythm of the trip at hand, this particular, unique trip. I begin to see new things, even on familiar roads; I get a sense of memories in the making, though for the life of me, I cannot often tell one trip from another.

And then the end: I get where I'm going for the time

being. This part has gotten less and less important to me the older I've gotten. It's become replaced in importance with the sense which comes earlier, and is at times ever so subtle, and at other times more like a moment of ecstasy, that I am somehow homeward bound, whatever the direction I'm travelling.

▲ We're All in This Together

"It's you, it's you I'm talkin' to."
—Bob Marley, *Coming In From the Cold*

Sometimes the sky seems so wide and seamless, so limitless and deep.

"Wyoming sky" is how my wife and I refer to it on days when there are no clouds in sight, the air is crystalline, and from horizon to horizon subtle color intensifies and wanes like the whispered passage of an immense faraway orchestra playing a single perfect note. Days like that seem to happen often in Wyoming. We were there on our honeymoon. We know.

Such a sky reminded me, recently, of how much we all are in the same boat as we go about our lives. I had just learned that a patient of mine had died, and I was crossing a lawn, numb, looking for someone to talk to. I felt empty.

It was a clear, brilliant winter day, and I looked around. Far to the east, hills and tall buildings stood at the edge of the horizon, against a light, electric edge. To the west, the low slopes of the Blue Ridge filtered dark through a grove of bare oaks, and the sky faded to white above them. Overhead, a cold sun shimmered through an immense and diffident blue canopy, ethereal and unreachable.

It wasn't until later, in my recollection of the morning, that I grew aware of how much I'd had a sense of each beating heart beneath that sky, and how lonely I felt because one soul I'd gotten to know a bit had moved beyond my knowing her more. While sharing life with millions of other people beneath a sky of immense beauty, I grieved the loss of a close collaborator in the intimate creativity that is psychotherapy.

Life is an act of collaboration from the get-go. For better or worse, we depend on each other for the substance and energy of our own very being, and in mixing it up with each other we gain the potential to create new life, whether in the form of babies, or insights, or paintings.

At the same time, we have equal potential, in our contact with each other, to harm the life we have in common. As a species we are alone in our capacity to destroy things which arguably go far beyond life: truth, honor, hope, creativity. I hope we are alone in the universe in this capacity.

If life thus consists of a dangerous kinship among human beings, artistic creativity is a dangerous and necessary kinship between artist and audience. Artist and audience meet in a unique encounter every time the work of an artist is experienced by another person, and both persons become equal co-authors of the uniqueness of the occasion.

Whether the experience is positive or negative depends on them both.

When is such an experience positive? In my book, it is when both artist and audience are more creative as a result of the encounter.

The dark side is that potentially, both artist and audience can have their creative energy diminished in the encounter as well.

There is an awkwardness here, however. In a sense, a hermit, solitary from birth, with no knowledge, or concept of other human beings, is potentially the most creative person on earth, in essence creating all things anew for himself.

And that is precisely the problem. Our hermit must, in essence, create all history for himself, and if he ever cares to venture far, must invent the wheel anew, as well as the cart to fasten it to. As to his audience, there is no possibility that anything from outside resources can be added. Like a tuning fork in a vacuum, such a person vibrates with no sound. Each vibration is new, but its productive potential is limited to the small, tight, and ultimately short-lived world of this one person.

Add one other person to this scene, though, and you've got a whole new show.

In isolation, two people who invent the wheel are likely both geniuses. If, however, they know of each other and choose to work separately to the same end, at least one of them is probably a bit of a fool—foolish because of the loss of a vast opportunity to use the synergy which is available when human beings are willing to engage with each other openly and use each other's creative work as a basis to extend into shared unknown areas rather than simply extending their own individual limits.

Very, very few human beings are isolated from others as a matter of circumstance, such as being imprisoned, or stranded on a desert island. However, most of us are isolated in some fashion from one another—by fear.

Most of us struggle at some point in our lives with fears of being judged inadequate, or incompetent, or undesirable by our fellows. We guard ourselves, often with exorbitant energy, against being hurt or rejected, and often avoid the riskier bits of life that could result in pain.

In art, what this translates into is that most of us would rather be audience than artist, and even then many of us are reluctant audiences.

I believe the reason for this is that there is a visceral quality to art that has to do with emotions more intense even than fear of physical pain. It has to do with a primitive fear of the unknown that surrounds us, that extends into the future beyond our deaths, and stands lurking at every turning in our relationships with each other.

Most of us only deal with this kind of fear when we feel we cannot avoid it, such as when we visit a family member

Essays on The Psychology of Creativity

in the hospital, or attend the funeral wake of a friend. At these times, our defenses are assailed, and we must witness the pain of people whose defenses are gone. In art, this fear confronts us with every brush or hammer or key stroke.

The guts it takes to let oneself be known as an artist, and in so doing to risk confronting this fear in public, makes being an expressive artist a relatively unusual undertaking in our society. Moreover, because it takes some of the same courage to be responsive to art as an audience, to witness the intimacy that art represents, even being an audience is somewhat unusual.

Enter the critic. Call this person teacher, or guide, or facilitator, his or her job—and the only task worthy of a good critic—is to allow artist and audience to encounter each other as fully as possible, and to learn from the experience. The measure of effective criticism is the extent to which the work of the critic encourages both artist and audience to keep participating in a creative process. The flaw in much of what passes for popular criticism today is an overemphasis on judgment of the art product rather than interpretation of the product as part of a creative process.

Let it be heard in every hall of education and throughout every school of criticism: have no tolerance for the pseudo-critical judgmentalism that turns what should be a permeable interface between artist and audience into a no-man's land where few dare venture toward new ground, and those who do are often torn up beyond all reason. Such criticism is as wrong in our society as a schoolteacher who thinks calling children "stupid" is a way to motivate them to become more intelligent. We no longer tolerate such abuse in our classrooms, and we should not tolerate it in our newspapers, magazines, or eleven o'clock news.

In the end, we are all in a creative process together, and we must hold each other to the highest of creative standards. Each of our words and deeds should encourage further creativity. If they do not do so, we should know that we have sinned.

▲ Awakening

It had been a busy month for me, and I was deeply involved in paperwork at the end of a long day when it dawned on me that I had forgotten to check the waiting room for my last appointment until the hour was almost up. I lurched to my feet and yelled "Oh, my God!" at the top of my voice in what I thought was an empty office building.

It wasn't.

Shortly, another therapist came out of her office, ashen-faced, expecting to find a dead body in the hallway or something equally unusual. What she found was me, frantically dialing away on a telephone and trying to reassure her that things were okay, under control, fine, just fine ... She thought I was crazy.

I hate to think what the patient sitting in her office thought.

My own patient had cancelled earlier that afternoon. We were both fortunate that she had done so. I was worn out.

That evening, I fell asleep before the sun went down, only to wake up at midnight bathed in the strange flickering glare of the television set. I turned it off and lay in the dark. I couldn't get back to sleep. I was overworked. I worried that I was stretching myself too thin, and in subtle ways conveying to my patients that I wasn't all there for them.

I needed a break. I needed my sleep. But my mind kept ticking over. I began to think about writing this essay. I thought of ideas for it, and how it would feel to be writing it. I thought of how nice it would be to have it all done.

My mind wandered again. I thought of our upcoming vacation and it occurred to me—like a revelation, so help me—

that I should take some painting materials with me.

I hadn't considered it. The idea of me in a townhouse on the Atlantic, touching away gingerly at pictures of dunes and surf, reminded me of the scene at the end of "The Godfather" where Marlon Brando is doddering about in his grape arbor and drops dead. I had been painting unsatisfactorily for several months, revisiting past ideas and playing with techniques and materials, without anything real gutsy happening. Frankly, I was feeling pretty feeble about my art at the moment.

What came to me next was a vivid set of memories of a painting I'd done in college, and the changes it had gone through over the years as I repainted parts of it. Elmer Bischoff, on a campus fly-by, had passed through the studio where I was working, and had politely spent some time looking at it.

Years later, when I saw his work for the first time, I thought I understood why that picture seemed remotely interesting to him at the time. I had been playing with a human figure as if it were a monument, and it had come out almost as a landscape in movement, a swirl of earth tones, yellows and reds and browns, a massive, naked, powerful, lumpy, slouching Moses moving toward a burning bush, with lines cropping the figure against the background.

I rolled over, next to my sleeping wife. I had the feeling I'd come back on to something—a direction—the hillocks and mounds of the human figure. The capturing and cropping of a human image as emotional architecture and landscape.

I tossed around some more, fitfully, uncomfortably.

I became aware that I was in the midst of what amounts to a creative fit for me. It's a bit like being surprised by an orgasm. I was like a bystander, privy to my thoughts and feelings, but detached from myself, observing, and fascinated. I began to feel energized rather than enervated.

It was enough, at that point, for me to do something

about it. I seldom do (and always kick myself later for not doing)—so this time, I got up to put my thoughts on paper.

And then images started occurring to me like popcorn popping. They flowed, like water from a tap, easily and effortlessly. I revelled. My mind was working like an instantaneous computer graphics program, shifting shapes and swapping colors with an abandon I'd misplaced long ago. I was on a high. Ideas! I was finally having ideas again!

And finally, it was enough. I crawled back into bed, and fell asleep like a baby. Life was good ...

Later: Having that burst of creative energy in the warm summer night was a long way from having this piece written as you see it now. It still took a past-due deadline and a lot of coffee to get it out of my head and into print. Having image after image popping into my mind in the still darkness was an emotional world away from having them down on stretched canvas; the yellows and ochres and reds in my imagination were much easier to mix in my head, and the underpaintings dried faster.

But, oh, the freedom of having the ideas! The knowledge that they existed, that I could be privy to them—it was so encouraging then, and now. And, while having the ideas alone wasn't sufficient, it's what it took for me to get moving. Slowly, and with inevitable changes, the pictures in my mind are coming into the light, and onto paper and canvas that others can see.

Creativity often seems to come at inconvenient times—when we're not expecting it, when we're tired or preoccupied, or hurried. Sometimes it shows up, as it did for me, in the middle of the night at the end of a hard day, expecting to be attended to like an eccentric friend who blows in from the coast on the spur of the moment.

On other occasions it stands quietly by the fringes of the action, waiting to be noticed, and obstinately refusing to call attention to itself, even when it is desperately clear we need it.

And sometimes, creativity is like a jealous lover who says, in effect, "It's her or me, big boy—pick *one* of us!"

Some of us *are* like monks or nuns, celibate to all but Art itself. But most of us keep our day jobs, and are peripatetic in our efforts to do it all, as artists and worker bees, *today*, *now*—but time is the ultimate limit here. And in the end, we do what we can. Some of us who dance with several partners become intimate slowly with each in turn. Some of us fail to get close to any at all.

Advice? Same as Joseph Campbell's. Pick your bliss. Then do what you must to spend time with it.

Last night I asked a painter, a watercolorist whose work I enjoy a lot, how he learned to do watercolor. "By doing a lot of watercolors," he said, the majority of which, by nature of the medium, failed. Every day, day after day, wherever he is, the guy does painting after painting—four to five hundred a year.

Nowadays, many of these are real beauties. If I were to ask him how long each one took him to make, the truest answer he could probably give me would be "Years."

▲ Free Association

"What comes to mind as you think about that?"

This question is one of the main tools used by many therapists, especially those trained in Freudian psychoanalytic theory, to trace the origins of a patient's thoughts, feelings, memories, and dreams. In a technique known as free association, patients are instructed to allow themselves to describe whatever thoughts or feelings enter their awareness, whether they make sense or not, or seem outrageous, improper, or unfair. By listening carefully, the analyst gets, in a sense, a guided tour of the patient's unconscious processes, and is often able to help the patient become aware of patterns and motivations which were out of his or her awareness.

The ability to associate ideas without censorship is a fundamental part of any creative process. In psychotherapy, the focus is on creative exploration of oneself and one's inner motivations. In other endeavors, the focus may be on the creation of new images, sounds, concepts, perceptions. In each case, however, the new work is a result of extending oneself into an area previously unknown.

What happens during the process of free association?

The intellectual safeguards and guidelines we normally use to screen out tangential ideas, to structure and control the development of concepts so they are reasonable, rational, and acceptable—these are abandoned deliberately. Instead, we give ourselves permission to be aware of each and every thought or feeling or idea that comes into consciousness, without judgment or immediate regard for its significance or contribution to the solution of a particular problem. We overcome our natural tendency to censor abhorrent ideas, to banish shocking or shameful thoughts—and instead, welcome them as a means of gaining information to understand things more thoroughly.

In free association, our thoughts follow no clear sequence—or at least, the sequence they follow is not immediately clear. They usually seem initially jumbled, unrelated or tangential at best, and in many occasions, absurd. We must often struggle with a sense of wasting time or effort in the process. We must tolerate the insecurity and fright that being directionless often draws out of us—a fear that is primitive in its origins, and corresponds to the dread of becoming "lost" that drives most young children to stay close to Mother.

Allowing oneself to associate freely, in therapy or out, is a difficult task for most people, at least initially. We do not easily give our minds free rein in today's world. It seems too risky. It takes courage and calls for trust in oneself. We crave order in our lives, for the most part. Boundaries and limits and guidelines provide us basic psychic comfort and reassure us of our self-control.

Moreover, there is another counterforce to freedom at work throughout our lives. We learn from early childhood to anticipate the impact of our thoughts, and to avoid or keep hidden the ideas which would be likely to damage our standing with people around us. More subtly, we learn very early to do the same with our own view of ourselves. Thoughts which endanger our self-esteem or make us ashamed of ourselves or frighten us are avoided, denied, or forgotten as soon as possible. In the jargon of psychoanalysis, from infancy on we develop a number of potent defense mechanisms for our psychic protection.

It is fascinating and instructive to recognize that these defense mechanisms serve us equally well in our interior lives as individuals, in our most intimate relationships with loved ones, and between us in the larger societies of the world. In fact, it is in the larger scope of behavior between nations that we can often see these mechanisms most clearly at work. We can study in the societal structure of countries the same characteristics which define psychopathology in individual human beings. Moreover, our frequent response to these defensive maneuvers, whether we become aware of them in ourselves, in our relationships, or in international affairs, is often similar: we are frustrated and angered by what feels like and is a denial of hidden truth.

This pursuit of hidden truth is a central activity of much human activity—certainly of psychoanalysis, political science ... and art. And freedom of association and expression is a vital component of each endeavor, both on the individual and societal level. For truth to emerge, we must have access to it in spite of the potential for our failure to understand it and in spite of our fear that the truth we learn will hurt. We must permit ourselves to connect disparate ideas, to explore tangents, and to speculate without clear purpose or direction. Censorship is, at every level, anathema to creativity.

We must also be willing to permit ourselves to err. This is probably the most important permission any person can give himself. Without it we are doomed to live a lie. "Neurosis seems to be a human privilege," as Freud observed; but the general task of neurosis, "defense against dangerous perceptions," is at odds with our need to know the world as it is, dangerous as it may be. By permitting ourselves to make mistakes, we allow ourselves to recognize that we make them. Thus, we can drop the defenses which so often distort our perceptions and we can appreciate the world from new perspectives.

Our lives are filled each minute with absurdity. Up against a deadline, with nothing in mind, I didn't want to waste time writing something stupid ... I simply wanted to finish this essay.

I wandered outside to play football with my son.

Bruce M. Holly

Football. Consider for a moment. How did the idea ever occur to anyone, much less a lot of people, that getting a group of large men together to hurt each other while chasing a lopsided ball across a field would be fun? For that matter, consider the literal absurdity of almost any sport people engage in. Consider tractor pulls. Consider mountain climbing. Consider ... nude Jello wrestling! I promise you, however, it took as much unique genius for these activities to emerge into human history as for the Pythagorean theorem to do so. It just so happened that at a critical juncture in time, the ideas involved and the person capable of combining them came together. As an exercise, try to imagine Pythagoras coming up with the sport of tennis. (Be careful to stretch a bit first, however.)

The point is, we live surrounded by ideas begging to be combined into revelations of unknown truth. Our daily lives are filled with the evidence of past combinations. Every cook worth his or her salt has tales from the kitchen of happy accidents which resulted in dishes that surprise and amaze. Good lovers have similar tales, from the laundry room to the hall closet. Vulcanized rubber, roast meat, oysters as an edible substance—all of these resulted from someone's unique willingness to associate the results of an accident or an error with the idea that those results could be useful or fun.

Each creative discovery takes someone to do it: to freely combine seemingly unrelated or discordant ideas; to push a concept one step further by imagining there is another step; to be willing to allow into awareness something that balances on the edge of the accepted reality of the time.

What comes to mind as you think about that?

▲ Opening Up

Creativity is an act of opening. Opening the eyes, the ears, the mind, the heart.

We float like gulls among the waves and currents of a wild foggy ocean of information and experience. Sometimes, the mist lifts around us enough to see a bit of the enormity and energy of what surrounds us. Most of the time, even a limited glimpse is enough to enthrall and terrify even the bravest among us.

We begin life in the midst of this ocean, surrounded by the seawater of our mothers' wombs. We emerge in due time to the light of day where the mists roll infinitesimally back with each moment we stay alive. Most of us learn to swim a bit as we grow, and thus we widen the area of our encounters. The courageous among us even learn to dive a little into the infinite depths below the surface of things. The gifted among us occasionally learn to soar high above, on the wings of our minds.

But the surface of life is where we usually stay, and where, for the most part, we encounter our brothers and sisters.

There are reasons for this. The surface is where the stuff of simple survival exists, and we are designed to survive, above all. Moreover, the surface of life, the ethereal interface between past and future we call the present, is where most of us feel safest, though this safety is clearly an illusion. Yet without the illusion, we could only quail in fear, waiting for our inevitable ends, or sink madly into rage at the monumental idiocy that thrust us into something as impossible as our lives.

But as surely as the sun comes, there are moments when each of us gets a fleeting glimpse of the universe around us, when the shroud of fog lifts unexpectedly from one of its mysteries, or an insight illuminates a layer of life beneath our everyday gaze, or in resting, our eyes behold a vision in the quiet stars above. Each of us has moments of epiphany, and in living, each of us must choose what we do with them.

It was a normal day. My son was down at the pond near our house doing something that initially involved a rocket engine and a model boat, and soon included a small frog, a very frightened deer, several trees, and a motorist on the nearby road. My daughter was at the word processor, programming a banner several feet long which said "Yippee, Mommy's Home!" in several languages. My wife was at work, and I was putting off some chores. I fell into a revery—I had, the night before, gone out for a farewell drink with a friend.

There are few things more exposing of one's self than the effort to make the most of a friendship that forms late. My friend had become a friend only in the past few months, after several years of acquaintance. Then he decided to relocate to a new state, and we found ourselves saying goodbye. We ended up talking about our lives in art as part of the process.

As we talked, I recognized why I enjoyed his company. I found myself bathing in a feeling of safety, and aware of a desire to let him know me as well as I could. I heard myself telling him something I discuss about as often as I chat about my sex life, which is to say, seldom: I told him how I find it almost impossible to accept being a student in art.

Pride, irrational self-expectations, and the fear of releasing hard-won illusions of competence are at the base of this, and they create an immense struggle within me which hinders every effort I make to develop skills and perceptions I need or want badly as an artist. I have had this struggle not only about art. As a young child, I refused to ride a horse at all, rather than be led on it the first time—I wasn't afraid of the horse, and I desperately wanted to ride; however, I expected myself to be able to ride horses as part of my innate being, and would not accept the notion that I could not do so without help. So too with climbing mountains—though I managed to disabuse myself of the notion that I knew innately what I was doing in that area rather quickly, thankfully before I died in my seamless stupidity.

I told him about a letter I'd received from another friend earlier in the day, in which she had described her own struggle with a demon that sounded remarkably similar to mine. "My own success is a tough act to follow," she had written. She spoke of how hard it was as an adult to allow herself to assume a "childlike position," as she put it, in permitting mistakes and failures as a means of growing. She then went further, and wrote of how, when her efforts got too "precious," in terms of effort, time, or materials, they could become frozen. Giving a large painting she had begun as an example of a work immobilized by too much investment, she said, "The process of creating it has been consumed by my need for a wonderful product."

Her way out, she described, was to take the attitude that she was simply out to make quick sketches of a moment when she painted, and to accept the flaws that each painting seemed to have as secondary to their ability to capture a fleeting instant for the future. And in doing so, she could move on.

And as I told my friend about the letter, I was aware it was helping me own up to my own fears.

The evening wore on. He told me about himself, and we both talked about envying each other's way of doing things. We found a lot of common ground. Finally, it was time to call it a night. I learned about him, and in his learning about me, I learned about myself.

That evening, I crept into bed realizing I'd been given a gift—a span of hours filled with insights I could spend years sorting out—all so subtle and underplayed that writing about them seems to make the emotions and feelings involved way too overstated. A kind of epiphany.

Art, at best, is a living language of epiphany, a record of the subtle telling gesture and texture so easily missed in the midst of the moment. It fills a human need to hear, and see, and feel the rhythms and high architecture of a music of the soul too easily lost in the ebb and surge of forces in the mist surrounding our conscious lives.

As artists, we are the divers and the flyers in the ocean of life, and it is on us to bring to the surface the visions we see and the music we hear in the deepest regions and highest ranges of our imagination. In doing so, we extend the lives of all our kind.

To do this, we must be willing to struggle with the fears and shames that limit our power to create. There is no better way I know of to help ourselves in these struggles than to share them with friends capable of creating safety in life's chaos by their willingness to accept us and listen, so we can hear ourselves.

There is an art to openness between human beings, and words between friends are a creative act as substantial as any sculpture. My friend is an artist whose work I esteem in this area.

He left the area a day after we spoke. My wife is amazed at how little I know of the "who, what, and where" of his life. I am amazed at how much I appreciate knowing the "why."

▲ Empathy

The best treatise on empathy in general, and empathy in art in particular, that I've come across yet is the coffee table art book by Betsy James Wyeth entitled *Wyeth at Kuerners*. In the book, Mrs. Wyeth collected drawings, watercolors, and tempera paintings done by her husband, Andrew, over more than forty years, as he studied the farm of a neighbor in Chadd's Ford, Pennsylvania. For more than four decades, Andrew Wyeth would frequently walk the mile or so to the Kuerner farm from his studio, and sketch or paint any one of a universe of scenes that presented themselves on this rather unremarkable little piece of the world. As a result, the visual understanding of the land and the couple who farmed it is breathtaking; more, it is a study in understanding Andrew Wyeth, the painter, by his wife—it is a book I spend hours in, late at night, when I want to understand people, artists, and art, better than I ever have before.

Empathy is what most of us need from each other. It is a state of sharing, of insight, of understanding, that provides the deepest possible form of healing and support between human beings. Empathy is the "walk in each other's shoes" that allows us to truly appreciate the full meaning of our human uniqueness.

Sympathy, on the other hand, is what most of us give each other in times of need. So what's the difference? What does it have to do with art?

Pay attention. Please. This is important stuff. Honest.

Emotionally, we tend to resonate to basic experiences in relatively similar ways. Within the constraints and guidelines of a given culture, and given the modest but necessary minimums of early parenting competence, most of us feel similarly on occasions that call forth joy, grief, terror, or outrage. In situations that are highly charged emotionally, we can predict fairly accurately what we, or others, are likely to feel. But—and this is a key point—even at these intense moments, no two persons ever experience things in exactly the same way. There are always subtle variations between people, even in the grossest of times.

In less clearly delineated, or more subtle types of situations, these individual differences become more marked, and less predictable. And it is these types of situations that make up the vast majority of human experience.

Sympathy is a response by one person to another's emotional experience which assumes that both would feel the same in a given situation. The first person imagines what the other is feeling, and responds to that, as if it were his or her own feeling. This is a process fraught with risk for inaccuracy. As Norman Paul described it in writing about the resolution of grief, a sympathizer "is principally absorbed in his own feelings as projected onto the object (of sympathy) and has little concern for the reality or validity of the other's special experience." Paul further commented that sympathy "bypasses real understanding of the other person; he becomes the subject's mirror image and is thus denied his own sense of being."

Why do we tend to give sympathy instead of empathy to each other at times of pain and loss, when we are most in need of real caring? I believe there are a number of reasons. Sympathy is a quick response; and it makes the giver feel better. There is often nothing else to give, short of taking the time to really experience the feelings of the other, as they really are, as uncomfortable and painful as that may be. And, frankly, most people shy away from being known that well, and out of common courtesy, we agree to draw a polite veil across the proceedings, by limiting our response. Finally, while sympathy often motivates us to benevolent and useful actions out of pity and compassion, subtly the transactions remind both the giver and receiver of who is hurt and who is not.

Empathy, on the other hand, is a process by which one person develops as deep and accurate an understanding as possible of another person's emotional experience and then experiences similar feelings. According to Dr. Paul, empathy presupposes the other person "as a separate individual, entitled to his own feelings, ideas, and emotional history." It develops between individuals as the result of communication with no prejudice as to what feelings should or shouldn't appear in a given experience.

Being empathic means being attentive, and accepting the existence of great intimacy. However, as Harold Pinter once wrote, "To enter into someone else's life is too frightening. To disclose to others the poverty within us is too fearsome a possibility." And as objects of empathy, most of us guard our inner picture of ourselves from public view—and present to the world doctored images of the persons we want to be. The dichotomy lives in the recesses of our consciousness, however, and for some, the result is a feeling of charade or charlatanship that colors every minute of our lives. Yet, to be understood, we must be willing to reveal ourselves, in some manner.

The absolute importance of communication in developing empathy is not to be lost. Empathy takes collaboration.

Many people make a distinction between empathy and sympathy by saying that one cannot empathize with another unless one has shared similar experience; i.e. men cannot empathize with childbirth, non-alcoholics cannot understand alcoholics, non-veterans cannot comprehend the experience of war veterans, and so on. I believe, however, that to base one's ability to understand on shared personal experience alone is folly.

While it is often easier to attend to important aspects of an experience by having gone through it oneself, this is not always the case. What is important to one person is often insignificant to someone else. While it is often easier to establish an emotional "shorthand" with which to describe an experience with someone who has shared similar events, even this is not a given. Each of us is too different, and our personal vocabulary for feeling is far too individual to be *a lingua franca*.

In the end, the recipe for empathy is this: find someone willing to describe his or her innermost feelings to you. Pay close and active attention, and be willing to see and feel the world as he or she does.

On the other hand, if you need to be understood, pick someone who knows how to go about understanding your experience, rather than someone who has simply had a similar one. Pick someone who listens well, and watches for the subtle unspoken language we all speak. Pick someone willing to go through the feelings you describe, not simply the ones he or she thinks are there. This advice applies to picking friends, lovers, parents, and therapists, by the way. And it applies to artists and audiences, too.

Artists are individuals who have accepted the task of being conscious and acting on their consciousness. According to R. G. Collingwood, in *Principles of Art*, "The artist's business is to express emotions." By being willing, and able, to express emotions so that others can perceive and understand them, artists serve society by allowing us as audience to learn about empathy without having to expose ourselves too directly to the raw emotions of real life. As audience, our involvement with the thoughts and feelings contained in art is defined and limited, and we are not asked, usually, to expose our own discomfort with life.

Art is a means of indirect experience for many, and is a catalyst for reliving and catharsis for some. As such, it demands courage and honesty from everyone involved—maker and viewer. As Collingwood noted, the artist among us "tells his audience, at risk of their displeasure, the secrets of their hearts." By so doing, we learn not merely to understand, but to appreciate our lives, and ourselves.

▲ Society and Creativity

Creativity is a process that is inevitable in the life of a human being.

However, as a result of our interactions with each other, the abilities we universally share as young children to be open and vibrant to the world around us most often decrease with time as our energies go more toward protecting ourselves and guarding against the pain and vulnerability that attend human relationships.

And as this happens, many of us lose much of our creative potential. This seems to be one of the truest and in the end saddest aspects of "normal" human development.

At the same time, as a race we *depend* on the individuals among us who remain creatively active to provide us with the visions and learnings that allow us to grow and improve our lot.

What a paradox—we tend to limit, by our societal attitudes and child-rearing, educational, and philosophical practices, the preservation and growth of the very process that makes us most fully human: our unique ability to create new realities in our lives and in the universe itself. And this tendency itself seems characteristically human: pervasive, at times purposeful, and always powerful, in whatever society has existed since the dawn of our days.

What news! The Family of Man is a dysfunctional family!

As surely as the family of an alcoholic suffers and struggles to find ways to cope with and minimize the damage done by drink, we humans struggle to protect ourselves from the frightening aspects of being alive. We form conspiracies of belief, organizing the facts of raw life into systems which give some order and coherence to what is going on. However, once formed, these systems of belief require protection themselves, for when questioned they often prove very fragile. We thus tend to avoid questioning what we culturally "know" because it would threaten whatever well-being we have gained. We deny the possibility that other systems are valid or, often, that they exist at all. And like members of an alcoholic family, we often highly resent our brothers and sisters who don't play along, who go their own way, or worst of all are willing to give whispered voice to the unmentionable, the classic elephants sitting ignored in the parlor: "Daddy drinks too much .... Daddy touches Susie .... Things could be different ...."

We adopt various postures as individual members of this Family of Man that are analogous to the roles taken by members of many alcoholic families. Some of us are "caretakers," taking responsibility for ourselves and our fellow family members, like alcoholics' spouses trying to repair the problems and damages wreaked by our mates in life, and living lives of often massive service to our fellows with often little or no acknowledgment. Some of us are "good children"—quiet, self-effacing, compliant, faceless, taking refuge in anonymity as we live out our lives. Others of us are the "rebellious ones," people who show the anger and pain that come from being hurt, but demonstrating it in self-injurious ways that in the end only yield further pain.

And some of us, a few, find the courage and resources to allow us to confront the notion that our family *is* in pain, and most crucially, that things *could* be different. In the family of an alcoholic, it is often only when such a person emerges and weathers the initial intense anger, fear, and resistance of other family members that change begins to occur. This person becomes a catalyst for improvement in his or her immediate family, and in terms of the potential change, serves as the catalyst for change throughout generations of the family yet to be born. In our society, these folks are the creative pioneers among us.

What can be done? How can our vast human family be helped? How can the healthiest aspect of our being, our creativity, be nurtured and stimulated rather than curtailed and thwarted as a matter of developmental course?

Silvano Arieti, a psychiatrist and student of creativity, speaks of a "creativogenic" society as one which promotes individual creativity in his 1976 book *Creativity: The Magic Synthesis*. According to Arieti, there are nine characteristics of such a society. The first, and most crucial, is availability of the cultural and physical means for an individual to be creative. Other characteristics include free access by all citizens to these means; at least a modicum of freedom from oppression; a cultural openness to stimuli and exposure to different and even contrasting stimuli; a focus on "becoming" rather than simply "being;" tolerance for and interest in diverging views; the interaction of significant, creative persons; and the promotion of incentives and rewards for creativity.

A society with these characteristics provides a fertile field for creative persons to produce. Such a society can encourage creativity, much like good soil can encourage good crops. But without people who will work this soil, planting the seeds of ideas and projects, looking ahead to when the seed bears fruit, both farms and societies remain creatively barren, no matter how rich they are in potential.

The United States is, by and large, a "creativogenic society." But we tend to treat many kinds of creativity with a great deal of disrespect. What are the characteristics of a creative person, and how are *these* characteristics to be fostered in *our* society?

Most students of creativity note these as common qualities among creatively productive people. They tend to be observant; willing to deal in half-knowing; willing to diverge from commonly held ideas; flexible; able to combine divergent, often opposing concepts; insightful regarding their own internal conflicts and willing to express these conflicts in some way; able to "play" with ideas without limiting self-criticism; and able to both concentrate on issues and range between apparently disparate ideas.

Most students of early childhood development, including most parents, would recognize those qualities as also common in most young children. The problem is, in the U.S. today, they are too often regarded as "childish," the immature functions of young minds which must ultimately be taught to conform and be productive, to think analytically and conventionally, and to avoid the frivolity and apparent uselessness of play and idle imagination.

Paul Torrance, in his writings about the relationship of education to creativity, made several recommendations for teachers who want to encourage creativity in children. In large measure, they are good advice for every parent, art and literary critic, and studio mate in this world. If we would help each other be creative, we should avoid making work and play two distinct activities; we should treat unusual ideas and unusual questions with respect; we ought to demonstrate to each other the intrinsic value of our ideas, support efforts at self-initiated learning, and encourage plenty of unevaluated learning and practice.

In essence, these ideas serve to preserve our potential for creative activity by preserving our ability to diverge from others in thought and perception. In general, each of us, from our days as toddlers onward, receive immense pressure to conform to the mainstream ideas, attitudes, and perceptions of the society we live in. We need all the help we can to be able to see and think and feel in our own unique ways, preserving this ability, which we shared in early childhood with most of our fellows, throughout our lives.

Bruce M. Holly

As a society, our professed values of independence, freedom, and tolerance are—as they are for many other things—good for creativity.

Our practice of these values in our homes, schools, and marketplaces must improve.

▲ IN THE MOOD

Dr. Ruth Richards, a psychiatrist on the faculty of the Harvard Medical School, recently summarized past and present research on the relationship between mood disorders and creativity in the *Harvard Mental Health Newsletter*. She made some interesting observations.

Moodiness has been linked with creativity throughout history. With the advent of systematic psychological research this link has been supported, often in startling ways. In some studies of eminent writers, for instance, as many as 80% of the subjects had a history of mood disorders. Most had what is now referred to as bipolar disorder, or manic-depressive illness.

Mania is a crazed, driven, intense state described as "going a hundred miles a minute," with overblown self-confidence and exaggerated and painfully urgent thoughts crashing like wild waves on one's mental shore, seeking escape more than coherent expression. Because of its intensity, it is a destructive and disruptive condition which causes major problems in everyday living for most sufferers. Suicide is a major risk for many. For some, a very few, this state and its opposite, a depression described best as an emotional black pit of hopelessness and despair, serve as sources of intensely rich fodder for creativity. The very intensity of these individuals' pain feeds monstrous talents which succeed in ordering and expressing the experience in coherent and monumental ways. Richards and others speculate that for these people, the driven energy of mania contributes to their ability to create "challenges to conventional thinking" and to produce unique and extremely creative work.

The passion of Blake, the rapture of Van Gogh—like runaway hearts which fuel superhuman feats, then break with the effort, mania drives and drains its hosts. The galleries of great creative accomplishment can in many cases be seen as mausoleums which honor the frantic, impossible efforts of persons doomed to burn out sooner rather than later. You might think of the condition as emotions on steroids.

For most sufferers, however, the peaks and depths of this mood disorder are too distorting as platforms for creative production, and the violence of the movement between these points is too draining to allow for the critical control necessary to hit the creative mark. What they are left with is life lived out of control, often with frequent swings between grandiose, frantic impotence and soul-searing depression. Fortunately, with recent developments in medicine and mental health there are treatments which allow many if not most people with manic-depressive illness to gain relief and to re-establish their lives successfully.

In her own research, Dr. Richards has concentrated on studying people with evidence of what she terms "everyday" creativity rather than artistic eminence. Her criteria for creativity simply included originality and meaningfulness to others; her subjects included auto mechanics, homemakers, entrepreneurs, teachers, and World War II resistance fighters.

Interestingly, Richards found that both the originality and the quantity of creative activity were highest among people diagnosed as manic-depressive or cyclothymic (a milder form of the disorder, with less extreme mood swings from elation to depression), and in the "normal" *relatives* of these individuals.

Other studies have had similar findings, with the common characteristic of the most creative subjects being that they were in a relatively mild state of elation, or elevated mood, called "hypomania" at least during some portion of their mood swings.

What is hypomania? It is clinically described as a marked elevation of one's mood, which does not impair one's ability to function: feeling "up," "turned on," excited, centered, focused, absorbed, energized. Most people can identify discrete periods of time when the way they feel fits this description. During these periods, people often experience their thinking as sharper, and their sensory awareness as more intense. Artists often recognize in this description the periods in which ideas flow more easily and more freely than any other time, and during which they are able to sustain creative effort with the greatest ease.

Hypomania is a condition that some seek to stimulate on demand by use of a variety of substances, especially stimulants. The problem here is that drug-induced elation is hard to keep "mild"—it tends to be weighted by a loss of critical judgment, and any heightened focus and speed of thought tends to be more illusion than fact. Just as humor is more complicated than the simple application of laughing gas, the mood that begets creativity is more than simply being "high."

Richards' work supports what seems obvious about the link between mood and creativity: when we feel "on," in synch with our surroundings, and excited by being alive, we tend to produce more original connections, think in broader, more inclusive terms, and solve problems more creatively. Up to a point, the more elevated our mood, the more we have access to "spontaneous exuberance" in Richards' words, and the more heightened is our "speed of thought, facility with new ideas, and ... sense of flow or welling forth of ideas." Combined with a capacity for abstract and coherent thought, feeling good can spark remarkable creative activity.

Moreover, the increased ability of individuals who experience elation, including the more intense versions of hypomania and mania, to be playful and to make up stories and strange combinations of ideas is a potential source of creative material. Further, it is a characteristic of playfulness that it is infectious. This may account for why the relatives of manic individuals often are remarkably creative themselves. There is very likely a systemic excitement of ideas going on in the exchange between members of the families in question.

The side implication here is, there is something to be said for hanging around with people who are excited or exciting, whether it is the result of general personality or the mood of the moment.

Creativity is kind of like a virus—it seems you *can* catch it from others.

▲ Turning On

Joseph Addison, an eighteenth century writer and publisher, once suggested that a "man that has a taste of musick, painting, or architecture, is like one that has another sense." In contrast, according to Thomas Huxley, for "a person uninstructed ... [life] is a walk through a gallery filled with wonderful works of art, nine-tenths of which have their faces turned to the wall."

A simple exercise, if you will. As you read this, become aware of the sounds and smells and textures and colors surrounding you ... the weight and balance and heft of this very book ... your posture ... the odd twinges and pressures and twitches of your body as you read ... the warmth or coolness of your surroundings. It is probably impossible for you to read the above passage without responding in some fashion to the suggestions. (If you didn't, I'd really like to hear from you.)

How did you do so? Through printed words on a page, you receive a suggestion of a direction to turn your attention, and as easily as shifting the lens of a camera or the microphone of a recorder, you do so. No mystery involved, but rather a simple matter of directing your focus.

It is interesting to note that the U.S. Army has codified this process over years. The art of paying close attention to one's surroundings under stress is taught by-the-numbers to thousands of recruits each year. Those who pay attention to the lesson often live to be grateful.

The point is, with few exceptions, we humans are born able to direct our attention, and it is possible to refine our skill into a most deliberate activity.

As an artist, have you ever noticed yourself looking at a

scene and making a conscious effort to understand what you see in terms of how you would paint or draw it? What happens?

- You begin to search for patterns and visual rhythms in the scene.
- You notice variations in light and shadow, and you see colors in terms of hue, value, and shade.
- You see shapes and relationships, and you notice where things are and where they aren't.

At the same time, you often become acutely aware of the other aspects of the situation: the smells and sounds, the warmth or cold surrounding you—and how these sensations influence your perceptions. If you keep at it, visual analogies to each of these sensations may occur to you.

And in due time you become aware of thoughts, feelings, and memories which emerge as you study and finally really *see* what's in front of you—echoes and ghosts of past experiences similar to the one you are immersed in at the moment.

In short, you become really alive and vividly awake to what's going on.

Furthermore, as the raw material for creative activity is forever and always in front of you, by simply being aware of it, you begin to be creative. For in the act of informing yourself, you are creating a new person.

This, I think, is most significant.

So much for creative blocks, in essence. For the person willing to turn on his or her "artist's eye," so to speak, creative work is already in progress.

"Artist's eye" has another equally valid name: "Survivor's eye." People thrust out to the edge of life itself by danger and disaster regularly report that at the moment of greatest stress, they find themselves most alive to the world around them. At these moments, this response serves a most useful defensive function—to survive in danger, one needs information. It is what keeps us from jumping out of frying pans into fires. In situations where our lives are on the line, our senses take on the keenest of edges, and awareness becomes autonomic for those of us who survive.

Interestingly, however, the same processes that click in automatically in times of danger are also available to us in less fearful moments. In fact, these processes often seem to occur without conscious effort at moments when we are at our most relaxed, as in the time before sleep or in the calm of simple contemplation.

In sum then, awareness is a natural process that can be refined by deliberate effort. It is not necessarily dependent on either high stress or deep relaxation, and it is within our conscious control. For the artist who keeps these thoughts in front of his or her mind, productive work becomes much more predictable, and fear of loss of the Muse becomes much less intimidating.

There are occasional kinks and vagaries in the system, to be sure. As with anything human, too much is too much. According to Daniel J. Boorstin in his book *The Creators*, Honore de Balzac made "every experience a point of departure" for creative work, writing ninety-two novels in his lifetime, while understandably complaining of his creative pace, writing fourteen to sixteen hours a day, six days a week. In a similar vein, Boorstin described Claude Monet as "almost an involuntary servant of optical impressions. Seeing his first wife on her deathbed, he could not prevent himself from capturing on canvas the blue, gray, and yellow tones of death on her face. Appalled, he compared himself to an animal who could not stop turning a millstone."

It is possible to be obsessive, in essence unable to focus or edit one's attention to the details of life, and compulsive in an attempt to gain some semblance of control or protection from the anxiety thus produced. Most of us fade in and out of this particular pathology at different periods in our development, and a miserable few of us get helplessly stuck in a minuscule focus which locks us into fruitless effort. But far more often, most of us find ourselves forgetting that by directing our attention to the subtle details of our daily life, we can gain a clearer, richer, deeper sense of understanding and mastery over the overall scene.

Nowhere more than in the creative act of viewing life with an artist's vision can we explore the texture and taste and hue and shade of feelings and thoughts which are no less a real part of every human experience than the earth we all stand upon.

Moreover, it is precisely by deliberately training ourselves to focus on the structure and rhythm and color that forms what we see that we can gain access to the emotional meaning that each scene contains.

By making sense of how to convert our visions into line and color on paper or shapes and shadows in sculpture, we enter into the purest of philosophy.

We begin to know, by seeing well.

▲ Comfort and Joy

Every night when I've finished work, I stop at a convenience store on my way home to get a cup of coffee. It's gotten to be a little ritual. I go in, check out the magazine stand, go to the coffee area, put some hot chocolate in the cup first, fill it up with coffee, and slurp off a little of the foam so I can get a plastic top on it. The lady at the register says, "Is that all?" I say, "Yup." I pay, and off I go.

I first started drinking coffee while I was in the Army. I remember figuring that if I could be drinking a cup of coffee, things couldn't be too bad. I was right. Now coffee is a bit like a secular sacrament to me. It makes me feel safe. I especially like driving with a cup of coffee in my hand. That feeling is worth a lot.

Sometimes, by the time I wind things up for the night, I have seen one person after another for six or seven hours straight. I don't usually feel tired—I feel like a gong, still ringing with the harmonic energy of a powerful concert recently ended.

For the most part, the folks I see are in the midst of dealing with or recovering from some very difficult and painful situations. They come in and for an hour or so each week, I provide them a safe place and an opportunity to be understood and accepted as they are. That's what I'm paid to do, and if I do it well, the experience often serves to help them see themselves and their lives in new ways, and to open new alternatives to them in what can be done to change things in the future. Don't ask me how it works. Any answer I gave you would be a guess.

But it does.

Sometimes folks come in hoping that I will be able to

offer *the* bit of advice that didn't get included in the buckets of advice most of them have already gotten from friends, family, their family doctor, or their priest, rabbi, or minister. They want the answer to how to make things different—how to make things better.

But usually, by the time I meet them, it is clear that advice isn't what is missing. It's something else.

Each person's story is different, and usually very complex. I never, ever get bored in my work. There are times, though, when I get scared, angry, delighted, awed—and very sad. There are times when I feel very useless, incompetent, empty, and furious at myself, at my inability to help. There are times when I can see nothing but the raw courage it takes some people just to stay alive. There are times I wish I could help my patients see things just a tiny bit differently—there are times I wish they weren't riveted so firmly to perceptions that seem so hurtful and distorted.

Pain in the world is like the air around us: if we want to live at all, we must go through it. The people I see know that, in spades. For some, life is like a yawning pit; pain is the only experience of living they can recognize from their pasts, their presents seem bleak, and it feels like there is no hope for change in the future. For others, the horses upon which they ride into therapy are problems like drinking too much, or the angry behavior of a son or daughter who is failing in school or in trouble with the law. For them, their sorrow seems like a fall from grace—the hopes for tomorrow that once seemed secure are fading fast into the ether, and helpless grief and anger seem the only possible responses. "One cannot be deeply responsive to the world without being saddened very often," Erich Fromm, a psychologist and author, once observed. Karl Menninger, a psychiatrist, further opined, "Unrest of spirit is a mark of life." For many of my patients, at least at first, life reeks of sadness and unrest of spirit.

But it was another psychologist, Norman Bradburn, who I think had a far more useful insight. He wrote, "It is the lack of joy in Mudville, rather than the presence of sorrow, that makes the difference."

Do not avoid sorrow. You can't. Instead, practice finding joy.

There it is, folks—the best recipe for living I know of. And I'll tell you what—I believe that for only one out of a thousand people is the doing of this almost impossible, and then it has almost certainly to do with a lack of awareness, rather than the lack of possibility.

Our book club recently read *Night*, by Elie Wiesel. It's quite a book.

Wiesel speaks of sadness: "In everyone's eyes was suffering drowned in tears."

Wiesel speaks of loss: "Never shall I forget that night ... which has turned my life into one long night, seven times cursed and seven times sealed .... Never shall I forget that nocturnal silence which deprived me, for all eternity, of the desire to live. Never shall I forget those moments which murdered my God and my soul and turned my dreams to dust."

Wiesel is describing his first night in Birkenau, the anteroom to Auschwitz.

Yet Wiesel speaks, in the midst of this hell, of happiness: "We did not yet know which was the better side, right or left; which road led to prison and which to the crematory. But for the moment I was happy. I was near my father."

Man's salvation is to be able to recognize, even in the throes of agony, the sources of joy that exist in *any* intimacy between ourselves and our brothers and sisters in life. Joy is not freedom from pain or fear or anger or want—it is the recognition that even in pain or fear or anger or want, someone somewhere cares about us. It is this recognition that allows people to emerge from despair; for couples at swordpoint to come together with new insight, or if need be, to live apart with respect for each other; for families at the brink of exploding to step back and try again.

For many of us, becoming aware of this caring is very hard. We often overlook it when it is there, or misinterpret it, resent it, deny it, avoid it. But it is there. If suffering is part of our humanity, so is caring. And as we flee suffering, we often flee the commitment that caring about each other implies. That, also, is human to do.

Here is where another component of our humanity, the creativity we all have as a potential strength, comes into play. If our tendency to pack it in and fold under pressure were dominant in our instincts as a species, humankind would long ago have disappeared from the earth. Why have we not? Because even in the hells we sometimes create for each other, we find ways to access the strengths we need to survive, not as animals, but as human beings, in every situation we are subjected to.

We alone among all life on this earth can go outside the lines of reason and instinct, creating new answers to old questions of survival as we go. We all have to be mad men and women to survive at times. And by allowing ourselves the madness of original thought, we can surmount whatever terror we face. It is how we find the joy we need to survive.

Theodore Rubin once wrote, "I must learn to love the fool in me—the one who feels too much, talks too much, takes too many chances .... It alone protects me against that utterly self-controlled, masterful tyrant whom I also harbor and who would rob me of human aliveness, humility, and dignity but for my fool."

May your fool meet my fool, and may we both find comfort and joy in the meeting.

Man, Dancing, Chalk on Paper,
24"x18", ©1978, Bruce Holly

Acrylic on Canvas,
12"x8", ©1994, Bruce Holly

▲ About the Author

Bruce Holly is an artist and psychotherapist with over twenty years of experience in addressing issues of creativity and human growth. He earned his B.A. at Notre Dame University, his M.A. at George Washington University, and his M.S.W. at Catholic University. He is Director of the Outpatient Clinic at Graydon Manor in Leesburg, Virginia and specializes in work with creative artists in a private practice.

A Contributing Editor to *Art Calendar* magazine, as the "Psychology of Creativity" columnist he addresses issues of creative block, confidence, dealing with criticism, and other important facets of the creative artist's inner life.

He enjoys sailing, skiing, mountaineering, making art, and traveling, and lives with his wife Jane, his son Blaise, and his daughter Lisa in Great Falls, Virginia.